# Duck & Waffle

# Duck & Waffle

## Recipes and Stories

## DANIEL DOHERTY

Photography by Anders Schønnemann

MITCHELL BEAZLEY

From a Crocodile to a Monkey

An Hachette UK Company
www.hachette.co.uk

First published in Great Britain in 2014
by Mitchell Beazley,
a division of Octopus Publishing Group Ltd
Endeavour House, 189 Shaftesbury Avenue
London WC2H 8JY
www.octopusbooks.co.uk
www.octopusbooksusa.com

Distributed in the US by Hachette Book Group USA
1290 Avenue of the Americas, 4th and 5th Floors,
New York, NY 10020

Distributed in Canada by Canadian Manda Group
664 Annette Street, Toronto,
Ontario, Canada M6S 2C8

ISBN 978 1 84533 957 9

Printed and bound in China
10 9 8 7 6 5 4 3 2 1

**Publisher** Alison Starling
**Senior Editor** Sybella Stephens
**Senior Art Editor** Juliette Norsworthy
**Home Economy & Food Styling** Annie Rigg
**Prop Styling** Liz Belton
**Senior Production Manager** Katherine Hockley

# Contents

The Duck & Waffle Story ................................. 6

Daniel Doherty's Food Philosophy ................... 10

Breakfast and Brunch ................................... 12

Small Plates .................................................. 50

For the Table ............................................... 124

Desserts ....................................................... 154

Snacks and Cocktails ................................... 184

Recipe Basics ............................................... 216

Index ............................................................ 220

Author's Acknowledgments ........................ 224

# The Duck & Waffle Story

To understand the Duck & Waffle story, you need to first understand a little
about the man behind the brand: Shimon Bokovza. Shimon and his partners,
Danielle Billera and Matthew Johnson, are the creators of Samba Brands Management,
the restaurant management company of Duck & Waffle, Sushi Samba, Sugarcane Raw
Bar Grill, and Bocce Bar. Shimon is the kind of man who only accepts yes for an answer

and, in doing so, he does the impossible. He is a trendsetter, innovator, and creative pioneer. For example, he opened Israel's first and only ski resort in 1969 at the tender age of 21. At that time it was new and fresh, and I bet many people told him he was crazy (which he is), but some things he just knows. He knows when to take a risk and follow his heart. He's a true visionary.

I had the pleasure of meeting Shimon at my previous job in Greenwich, where he instantaneously mesmerized me. While he often looked tired from traveling, the man was intense, driven, and never missed a beat. I find it very difficult to write about him, as even now I still don't fully understand him. He has the attributes of a wonderful father, evident in the way he mentors people, from his ability to recognize and shape raw talent to his sheer honesty as he guides his team to meet expectations they would otherwise never attempt. He is quite simply one of the greatest individuals I have had the pleasure of working with. When someone like that is leading your team, anything is possible. You get the confidence to try new things and the thought of failure doesn't provoke fear. I can honestly say, with my hand on my heart, that I never want to work for anyone else.

It's hard to imagine that only two years ago I was trying to explain to my wife why I had accepted a job from a guy I barely knew, at a restaurant with no name, and with a first assignment to fly to Miami for two months to develop menus. I'm not usually that type of guy. I like my life to

be methodical, but I had such a great feeling about this endeavor because of Shimon's confidence and charisma. Sure enough, two weeks into my visit to Miami he was telling me that the restaurant would be called Duck & Waffle and would operate 24/7 in a part of London infamous for being dead during the weekend. I thought he must be nuts—but he was right. We were, and have been, full from the beginning: 6 A.M. to 3 A.M. most nights, and all the way through on others. The name is cool, and the philosophy behind the restaurant is wonderful.

I spent almost two months in Miami working with Timon Balloo, Executive Chef of Sugarcane Raw Bar Grill. He's one of the most naturally talented chefs I have met and had the pleasure of cooking with. At the time, Sugarcane was Samba Brands Management's only non-Sushi Samba restaurant, and it has received great critical acclaim since opening in January 2010. I'd have taken any job in Timon's kitchen if I hadn't been due to open the restaurant in London. We cooked together, got to know each other, and tried to figure

out how we could transfer the success of Sugarcane to London. Luckily, we had a very similar outlook on food, so that part was easy. The menu was super seasonal, based on the simple components of sweet contrasted with salty, savory, and sour textures. It sounds fairly straightforward, but nobody understands this better than Timon.

Upon seeing the magnitude of the space in Heron Tower, Shimon decided to open two restaurants instead of just Sushi Samba. The 40th floor would be the home of another concept, whether inspired by Sugarcane or something else entirely. Sounds like a challenge, right? But that wasn't daunting enough for Shimon. Prior to Duck & Waffle, there was only one other 24-hour restaurant in London, so logically it would be yours truly who was tasked with creating another...on top of a skyscraper with crispy duck and waffles, but alas, I believed in it.

It was Danielle, the aforementioned managing partner and wife of Shimon—the sanity of the company—with her cool reason and calm intelligence, who suggested

naming the restaurant after Timon's best-selling dish on the Sugarcane menu: duck and waffle. And what an idea that was! It has had a significant impact on London's culinary scene.

Today, Shimon is as present as ever—be it on the phone or stomping around the kitchen stealing nuts—and he still tells me whether a dish is great, good, or sucks. He pulls no punches and is straight to the point. We continue to better ourselves, to evolve, and to build on what we have from within, using the great talents of the team. We are very lucky to have so many people, staff and guests, who believe in us, and in what we are trying to accomplish.

Of course, like any chef I have targets to hit and costs to monitor, but my sole calling is to cook and create, and that's the best feeling a chef can have. This book is not only a window into what we do at Duck & Waffle, but also a testament to each and every member of our team who has made the seemingly impossible possible, and that includes our wonderful guests, too.

I can't wait to see you in the clouds!

# Daniel Doherty's Food Philosophy

Often people ask me what type of restaurant we are and what kind of food we do. The truth is I don't really know, and I don't think I ever will. I don't think that's necessarily a bad thing—we just cook seasonal food in a style that we think suits it best. Even though the menu includes many different cultures, we never mix them on the plate. The best phrase I could think of when asked by a journalist was "often traditional, sometimes playful," which I think is fairly accurate. It's what best describes my cooking style and me. Whole roast Sunday chicken versus spicy ox cheek doughnut, baozi with bacon jam versus pea and ham soup. It's all about balance—I think you need some playfulness in life, but too much and it's overkill. As long as you take beautiful produce, at its peak, and cook it with love, you really can't go wrong.

When it comes to ingredients, I feel you must start with the basics. Good salt, extra virgin olive oil, real bread, natural vegetables, well-reared meat, and fresh fish. If you don't start with those, you really have nothing. Seeing the love and passion that goes into making olive oil, the rigorous tastings, the variation from each country, region, producer, and olive, is fascinating, and is reflected in all kinds of food production. Lord Newborough at Rhug Estate is a wonderful man, a man who doesn't compromise the quality of his organic meat, no matter the financial strain, and there are growers all over the country who feel the same about their beets or their carrots, bakers driving themselves crazy over making the perfect bread, and so on. If food doesn't make you excited in its rustic form, forget about refining it.

As the great Fergus Henderson says, "Don't be afraid of your ingredients or they will misbehave." He also said, "Britain is blessed with short, wonderful seasons. Just pay attention and nature will write a menu for you."

More important than any of the above is that you enjoy eating. One of my favorite things to do at work is to watch our guests from the open kitchen, and see their expressions. There is nothing more satisfying than seeing someone have a "moment" when eating your food. As American writer Harriet van Horne once said, "Cooking is like love; it should be entered into with abandon or not at all."

BREAKFAST AND BRUNCH

This is a healthy start to the day. The granola can be batch-made and kept in your bread box, and the compote can be batch-made and frozen in smaller portions. This is what we eat at the restaurant most days, as one simply can't eat duck eggs baked in cream every day...although we do sometimes slip off the wagon.

# Greek Yogurt with Homemade Granola and Fruit Compote

**Serves:** 2

**Preparation time:** 15 minutes (if the granola is ready-made), plus cooling

**Cooking time:** 20 minutes

1 cup organic Greek yogurt

¼ cup Granola
(see page 218)

¼ cup Fruit Compote
(see below) or fresh fruit

**For the fruit compote**

2 pints (about 4 cups) mixed summer berries

¼ cup superfine sugar

1 star anise

juice of 1 orange

To make the compote, put the fruit into a saucepan with the sugar, star anise, and orange juice. Place over medium heat, bring to a boil, then lower the heat and simmer for approximately 20 minutes, or until the liquid has reduced and you are left with a thick mixture. Let cool, then refrigerate until you are ready to use it. Any leftover compote can either be frozen, or stored in a sealed plastic container in the fridge for up to 1 week.

To serve, simply layer the yogurt, granola, and compote in a bowl and enjoy!

Having a free-flowing supply of waffles meant we just had to offer a sweet version. This is one of our most successful combinations. Others that have worked really well are summer berries with Chantilly cream, and caramelized apples, toffee sauce, and cinnamon ice cream. The variations are endless, so be creative and adventurous. I recommend making the chocolate hazelnut spread instead of buying it—it lasts for ages if stored in the fridge, and is worth the effort!

# Sweet Belgian Waffles

**Serves:** 2
**Preparation time:** 45 minutes
**Cooking time:** 15 minutes

oil, for brushing

half batch of Waffle Mix (see page 140)

2 bananas

superfine sugar, for dusting

2 scoops of Vanilla Ice Cream (see page 219)

**For the chocolate hazelnut spread**

scant ½ cup hazelnuts

½ cup powdered sugar

2 teaspoons unsweetened cocoa powder

¼ cup drinking chocolate

1¾ ounces baking chocolate (65% cocoa solids), melted

1 tablespoon canola oil

⅓ cup water

**For the peanut crunch**

½ cup superfine sugar

a splash of water

⅓ cup peanuts

You will also need a waffle iron

To make the chocolate hazelnut spread, preheat your oven to 350°F. Put the hazelnuts on a baking pan and roast until golden (approximately 5 minutes). Place in a food processor and blend until ground. Add the powdered sugar, cocoa powder, and drinking chocolate and blend together, then add the melted chocolate and blend for about 5 minutes. Gradually add the oil and water.

To make the peanut crunch, put the sugar and water into a saucepan over medium heat and cook until it becomes a caramel. Add the peanuts and mix well, then turn out onto a cookie sheet lined with nonstick parchment paper. Allow to set, then smash into small pieces using the end of a rolling pin.

When ready to serve, turn on your waffle iron and cook the waffles. Brush the hot waffle iron with oil and pour a ladle of batter into each mold. Spread it all around because the batter is quite thick and won't spread on its own. Cook until golden and cooked through, about 3 minutes.

Split the bananas in half lengthwise, dust with a couple of pinches of superfine sugar, and caramelize with a kitchen blowtorch.

To serve, build up each dish with a waffle on the bottom, then a good spoonful of hazelnut spread, then the bananas and the ice cream. Finally, scatter the waffles with the peanut crunch.

We created the Dossant after being inspired by New York's Cronut, which was dreamed up by Dominique Ansell, who started a craze with the first croissant/doughnut hybrid. Instead of making a doughnut-shaped croissant, we cook and fill a croissant like a doughnut. You can play around with the flavors as you get more confident with making the crème pâtissière. You can also try making the croissants from scratch, but it's quite tricky, and using frozen ones is fine.

# Dossants with Coffee and Amaretto

**Makes:** 8

**Preparation time:** 2 hours

**Cooking time:** 30 minutes

vegetable oil, for deep-frying

8 croissants (frozen is fine, but they must be uncooked)

½ cup superfine sugar, for rolling

nibbed or sliced almonds, toasted, to garnish

### For the crème pâtissière

1 cup milk

1¾ cups heavy cream

1 vanilla bean, seeds only

1 egg

3 egg yolks

scant ½ cup cornstarch

½ cup + 2 tablespoons superfine sugar

1 double espresso

1 tablespoon Amaretto liqueur

### For the almond crunch

½ cup superfine sugar

2 tablespoons water

½ cup sliced almonds

You will also need a deep-fat fryer and a pastry bag

The crème pâtissière should be made in advance, as it needs time to cool. Put the milk, cream, and vanilla seeds into a saucepan and heat to just below boiling point. Meanwhile, mix the egg, egg yolks, cornstarch, and sugar in a bowl. When the milk and cream mixture is hot, pour it slowly into the bowl of eggs, while whisking. Return the mixture to the pan and lower the heat. Continue to stir until it thickens to a consistency like mayonnaise, taking care that it doesn't stick to the bottom of the pan or scramble.

Pass the mixture through a sieve, using a spatula to push it through, which will result in a thick silky custard. Put a layer of plastic wrap directly on top so a skin doesn't form, and set aside to cool.

Next, make the almond crunch. Put the sugar and water into a saucepan over medium heat and cook until it becomes a caramel. Add the nuts and mix well, then turn out onto a baking pan lined with nonstick parchment paper and let cool. When cool it will be hard, so smash it into pieces with a rolling pin. Store in a dry place, but not in the fridge.

When ready to cook and serve, heat the oil to 320°F in your deep-fat fryer and drop in your frozen croissants. How long you cook them for will depend on their size—a normal croissant will take about 20 minutes, turning every 4 to 5 minutes, and a mini one (about one-third of the size) will take 10 minutes.

While the croissants are cooking, add the coffee and Amaretto to the crème pâtissière and beat well. Spoon into a pastry bag.

When the croissants are ready, take them out of the fryer and let them drain on paper towels. Roll them in the superfine sugar, then make a cut all the way down one side. Pipe in the crème pâtissière and sprinkle with the almond crunch and the toasted almonds. Eat immediately for maximum effect.

This is a recipe I picked up in Miami, and it's now our top-selling breakfast dish. Back in March 2012, when I was working at our sister restaurant Sugarcane, in Midtown Miami, one of the Colombian chefs was making breakfast to aid his tender feeling after quite a heavy night. He told us about a dish called "perico," based on scrambled eggs, scallions, and tomatoes, which he loves to eat when hung over. I loved the lightness of it—in the UK we tend to go heavy when in need of some TLC, but this was light, and vegetarian. I added some ripe avocado and put the whole thing on toast, and a winner was born. At the restaurant we offer grilled chorizo sausage or smoked salmon as an add-on.

# Colombian Eggs

**Serves:** 2

**Preparation time:** 10 minutes

**Cooking time:** 5 minutes

1½ tablespoons unsalted butter

2 scallions, finely sliced on an angle

4 eggs, beaten

1 plum tomato, quartered, seeded, and cut into ½-inch dice

sea salt and freshly ground black pepper

2 slices of sourdough bread

1 ripe avocado, cut into slices ¼ inch thick

Melt the butter in a skillet. When it's foaming, add the scallions and cook until soft, taking care not to let them burn.

Add the eggs and scramble lightly. Finish with the diced tomatoes and season with salt and pepper.

Toast the sourdough and lay the avocado on top. Spoon the eggs onto the avocado, season again, and serve.

Pearl barley is a great ingredient, and one that we use a lot in the restaurant. It's super healthy, and can be used in many ways. This is one of our signature dishes, and I've also given a variation that I sometimes eat for lunch.

# Pearl Barley Ragout with Goat Curd and a Fried Egg

**Serves:** 4

**Preparation time:** 20 minutes, plus soaking

**Cooking time:** 1 hour

3 tablespoons olive oil, plus extra for frying the eggs

2 onions, minced

2 garlic cloves, minced

1 bay leaf

1 sprig of fresh thyme

1 cup barley, soaked overnight in cold water

1¼ cups vegetable stock or Chicken Stock (see page 216)

2 tablespoons unsalted butter, plus extra for frying the eggs

2 handfuls of mixed wild mushrooms

sea salt and freshly ground black pepper

1 ounce Confit Shallots (see page 217)

4 eggs

2 sprigs of fresh parsley, chopped

2 sprigs of fresh cilantro, chopped

¼ cup goat curd

Balsamic Glaze (see page 217), to finish (optional)

First you need to cook the barley. Once cooked, it can stay in the fridge for up to 3 days.

Heat the 3 tablespoons oil in a large saucepan. Add the onions, garlic, bay leaf, and thyme, and cook gently for 5 to 10 minutes, or until they start to soften. Drain the soaked barley and add to the pan. Mix well and slowly add the stock, as if you were making a risotto. Once all the stock is used and absorbed, pour the barley onto a baking pan lined with nonstick parchment paper, removing the thyme and bay leaf, and let cool. At this point you can refrigerate the barley and save it for later.

When ready to eat, heat a skillet and add the butter. When it's foaming, add the mushrooms and sauté for 3 to 4 minutes. Season with salt and pepper, then add the barley and give it a good shake in the pan. Continue to sauté for 5 minutes. Add the confit shallots and correct the seasoning.

At this point, heat a drizzle of olive oil in a large skillet, and when hot, add a walnut-sized lump of butter. When it begins to foam, add the eggs, season with salt and pepper, and gently fry for 2 to 3 minutes. If you like them well done, flip the eggs over to seal the tops.

Finish the barley ragout with the parsley and cilantro. Place 1 tablespoon of goat curd on each serving plate, and spread it out. Divide the barley between the plates, and place a fried egg on top of each serving. Finish each plate with a little balsamic glaze (see page 217) if you like.

**VARIATION**

Try swapping the wild mushrooms and goat curd for Peperonata (see page 59) and chorizo. Peel the casing off of 3 cooked smoked chorizo sausages and dice them into ½-inch cubes. Sauté for a couple of minutes so that the natural oils come out, then add the barley and, after cooking together for 3 to 4 minutes, fold through the peperonata and finish with an egg.

This is one of our most luxurious breakfast dishes, perfect at the end of a hard night or as a treat on a Sunday morning. You can play around with the ingredients you use—a layer of spinach at the bottom of the dish is a good addition, as is diced smoked haddock in place of the mushrooms. It also makes a nice appetizer.

# Duck Egg en Cocotte with Wild Mushrooms and Gruyère Cheese

**Serves:** 2
**Preparation time:** 10 minutes
**Cooking time:** 30 minutes

butter, for greasing

1 tablespoon olive oil

2 shallots, minced

1 sprig of fresh thyme

½ a garlic clove

1 bay leaf

1 handful of wild mushrooms, roughly chopped into ¾-inch pieces

½ a glass of white wine

½ cup + 2 tablespoons heavy cream

sea salt and freshly ground black pepper

2 duck eggs

2 slices of sourdough bread

3 tablespoons shredded Gruyère cheese

3 to 5 truffle slices per person

Butter the insides of two 3-inch ramekins or individual cocottes.

Heat the olive oil in a saucepan and cook the shallots with the thyme, garlic, and bay leaf until softened. Add the mushrooms and cook for 5 minutes more, then add the wine and simmer until reduced by three-quarters. Add the cream and continue to cook until reduced by half, then season with salt and pepper.

When ready to serve, preheat your oven to 350°F.

Place half of the sauce in the bottom of each ramekin, removing the thyme and bay leaf, then crack a duck egg into each. Top with the rest of the sauce, and place in the oven for 3 minutes.

Toast the bread and cut into fingers. When the 3 minutes are up, or the whites have started to form, add the cheese to the ramekins and cook for a further 4 to 8 minutes, depending on how well you like your eggs cooked.

Garnish with the truffle slices and serve immediately with the toast fingers.

Smoked haddock and English mustard go really well together, and are both wonderful British ingredients. The inspiration came from the dish Omelet Arnold Bennett, named after a writer who requested smoked haddock omelet with Gruyère every time he stayed at the Savoy hotel, in London, in the late 1890s.

# Smoked Haddock with Hash Browns and English Mustard Cream

**Serves:** 2

**Preparation time:** 10 minutes

**Cooking time:** 30 minutes

14 ounces smoked haddock, skinned (reserve the skin)

2 potatoes, skin left on, parboiled so they are 50% cooked

1 bunch of scallions

sea salt and freshly ground black pepper

2 cups milk

2 cloves

2 sprigs of fresh thyme

1 bay leaf

1 tablespoon olive oil

2 shallots, minced

1 glass of white wine

scant 1 cup Chicken Stock (see page 216)

scant 1 cup heavy cream

1 tablespoon English mustard

a squeeze of lemon juice

vegetable oil, for shallow-frying

2 eggs

Cut the haddock into 2 portions and set aside.

Grate the potatoes and mince the scallions. Mix together and season with salt and pepper. Shape into 4 hash browns, and set aside until ready to serve.

Put the milk, cloves, 1 sprig of thyme, and the bay leaf into a medium saucepan and bring slowly to a boil. Add a pinch of salt, then lower the heat for 10 minutes to let the flavors infuse the milk. Strain into another saucepan and set aside.

To make the sauce, put the olive oil, shallots, the other sprig of thyme, and the haddock skin into a saucepan and cook gently for 8 to 10 minutes, or until soft but with no color. Add the wine and simmer until reduced by three-quarters, then add the chicken stock and continue to simmer until reduced by half. Add the cream, season with salt and pepper, and bring to a boil, then lower the heat again and simmer until thick. Whisk in the mustard and lemon juice, then strain.

When ready to serve, warm the milk over medium heat and add the haddock. After 6 minutes it should be cooked. Meanwhile, shallow-fry the hash browns in a little vegetable oil for 2 to 3 minutes each side, or until cooked, then poach your eggs.

Serve each piece of haddock with an egg on top, with 2 to 3 tablespoons of sauce spooned over, and the hash browns on the side.

In America this is called "toad in the hole," and in New Zealand it's "frog in the pond," but for obvious reasons we couldn't use the first name, and the latter didn't feel right, so we created our own name: "egg in a basket." This is my idea of a perfect brunch dish, and it's one I regularly cook at home, too.

# Duck Egg in a Brioche Basket

**Serves:** 2
**Preparation time:** 5 minutes
**Cooking time:** 10 minutes

2 tablespoons olive oil

2 slices of brioche, 1-inch thick

2 duck eggs

scant ½ cup shredded Gruyère cheese

1½ tablespoons butter

3 to 5 truffle slices per person

6 small fresh basil leaves

sea salt and freshly ground black pepper

1 handful of watercress

2 tablespoons Sherry Dressing (see page 215)

Preheat your oven to 320°F.

Heat the olive oil in a large ovenproof skillet over medium heat. Using a round cookie cutter, cut a 2-inch hole in the center of each slice of brioche. Add the brioche to the pan, and crack a duck egg into the middle of each one. Let the eggs start cooking on the bottom.

As soon as the white starts to get firm, scatter the cheese all over both brioche slices and add the butter to the pan. Place in the oven for approximately 3 to 6 minutes, depending how you like your eggs—the cheese should be melted but the yolk should still be runny.

Garnish with the truffle slices and basil leaves, season with salt and pepper, and serve with the watercress, drizzled with the sherry dressing, on the side.

As if this recipe isn't enough, we also have the Fat Boy variation, where we add maple-glazed bacon and a fried duck egg to the sandwich. Sounds weird, but trust me. Just make sure you go and take a nap afterward.

# Toasted PBJ with Banana and Berries

**Makes:** 2
**Preparation time:** 10 minutes
**Cooking time:** 15 minutes

4 slices of brioche, ¾ inch thick
2 tablespoons strawberry jam
2 tablespoons peanut butter
2 bananas, cut into ¼-inch slices
½ stick unsalted butter, divided
scant 1 cup heavy cream
3½ tablespoons superfine sugar
seeds from ½ a vanilla bean
2 small handfuls of mixed seasonal berries
powdered sugar, for dusting

Preheat your oven to 320°F.

Spread 2 slices of brioche with the jam, and the other 2 with the peanut butter. Add the sliced banana to the jam slices and put the peanut butter slices on top, to make 2 sandwiches.

Heat an ovenproof skillet and add half the butter. When it starts foaming, add the sandwiches and cook over medium heat until golden brown. Turn them over and add the rest of the butter, then place the pan in the oven for approximately 10 minutes, or until golden on top and warm inside.

In the meantime, whip the cream, sugar, and vanilla seeds to soft peak stage.

Take out the sandwiches, place on a cutting board and cut them in half. Serve with a dollop of whipped cream and the seasonal berries on top, and dusted with powdered sugar.

Beans on toast is a British staple, and I felt obliged to reinvent it. When I was at school, I had a part-time job in a restaurant in my hometown, Shrewsbury, which became full-time during the summer vacation. On my split shifts, I'd pop home and, without fail, have two slices of toast with beans and cheese on top. I'll never forget those moments between manic shifts where holding a knife was daunting, and I think about it every time we serve this dish.

# Beans on Toast

**Serves:** 4 to 6

**Preparation time:** 20 minutes, plus cooling

**Cooking time:** 3½ hours

1 cup dried white beans, soaked overnight, or 2 cups ready-to-go cooked beans

1¼ cups passata (thick tomato purée)

1 onion, minced

2 garlic cloves, crushed

1 sprig of fresh thyme

1 sprig of fresh rosemary

1 bay leaf

1 smoked ham hock

1¼ cups Chicken Stock (see page 216)

2 chipotles en adobo from a jar

⅓ cup dark brown sugar

1 tablespoon paprika

sea salt and freshly ground black pepper

2 tablespoons Bacon Jam (see page 200)

1 cup shredded extra sharp Cheddar cheese

sourdough bread, toasted, to serve

Preheat your oven to 320°F.

Place all the ingredients apart from the bacon jam, cheese, and toast into a Dutch oven and cover with the lid. Place in the oven for a good 3 to 3½ hours, or until the hock gives way under a gentle push with a fork. If using ready-to-go beans, add them an hour before the hock is ready.

When this stage is reached, remove from the oven, and let cool. Take out the ham hock and remove the skin, then shred the meat with your fingers and put it back into the Dutch oven with the beans.

At this stage you can chill the dish, or bring it back up to temperature to serve. If serving now, turn on your broiler. Heat up the bacon jam, and toast your bread.

When the beans are hot, transfer them to a baking dish and top with the cheese. Place under the broiler to melt and brown.

To serve, spread the bacon jam on the toast, and add a good ladleful of beans on top.

Here's another dish that can soothe your pains, one which, with the addition of one or all of the three magical ingredients (bacon, cheese, and hot sauce), can further aid your recovery. This is the kind of food we have found people tend to look for around the 4 A.M. mark, but it also works as a post-sleep cure.

# Salt Beef Hash with Poached Egg and Hollandaise

**Makes:** 2 hangover-size portions
**Preparation time:** 45 minutes, plus cooling
**Cooking time:** 3 hours

olive oil

10 new potatoes, cooked and halved

sea salt and freshly ground black pepper

2 tablespoons Confit Shallots (see page 217)

2 eggs

2 dill pickles, sliced ¼ inch thick

**For the beef**

1 piece (approximately 1 pound 2 ounces) salt beef

1 onion, peeled and halved

1 bay leaf

1 carrot, peeled and split in half lengthwise

**For the hollandaise**

2 tablespoons white wine

2 tablespoons white wine vinegar

2 peppercorns

1 sprig of fresh thyme

2 egg yolks

2¼ sticks unsalted butter, clarified (heated so the fats and milks separate—discard the milks)

1 tablespoon English mustard

1 squeeze of lemon juice

Place the salt beef in a medium saucepan. Cover with cold water, and add the onion, bay leaf, and carrot. Bring to a boil, then lower the heat and let simmer for approximately 2½ hours, or until the beef gives when pushed with the back of a spoon. Let cool in the stock. When cool, cut into ¼-inch slices.

Preheat your oven to 350°F, and bring a saucepan of water to a boil.

Heat a splash of olive oil in an ovenproof skillet and add the potatoes and salt beef. Season with salt and pepper. Once sizzling, put the pan into the oven for about 10 minutes, or until the beef starts to become golden brown.

Next, make the hollandaise. Put the wine, vinegar, peppercorns, and thyme into a small saucepan and bring to a boil. Reduce the heat and simmer until reduced by half, then strain into a bowl. Add the egg yolks, and whisk over a saucepan of simmering water until light and fluffy. This should take around 5 minutes. If the water starts to boil below the bowl, turn off the heat—there will be enough heat in the pan to cook the eggs, but just be careful they don't scramble.

Very slowly start adding the clarified butter while whisking constantly, until the mixture has a consistency like mayonnaise. If it gets too thick, adding a teaspoon of warm water will bring it back to life. Stir in the mustard and lemon juice. The hollandaise will hold in a warm place for at least 30 minutes—next to your stove should be fine. Just be careful it's not too warm or it may split.

Remove the hash from the oven, and add the confit shallots. Give it a little sauté on the stove for a further 5 minutes.

At this point poach your eggs, keeping an eye on your hollandaise.

Place the salt beef hash onto plates and add the pickles. Serve the poached eggs on top, season with pepper, and give them a good coating of hollandaise.

A hash that involves potato, spicy pork, and onions, topped with a runny egg and cheese, is my perfect hangover cure. I also like to add a few splashes of hot sauce at the end, to really blow out the toxins. You will need a sleep afterward; it's part of the recipe after all.

# Hangover Hash

**Serves:** 2

**Preparation time:** 20 minutes, plus cooling

**Cooking time:** 2 hours

**Resting time:** 1 hour's sleep

10 new potatoes

sea salt

1 x 4½-inch cooked smoked chorizo sausage, cut into ½-inch dice

olive oil

2 tablespoons Peperonata (see page 59)

2 eggs

1 cup shredded Gruyère cheese

sea salt and freshly ground black pepper

**For the onion jam**

3 tablespoons olive oil

2 large onions, finely sliced

1 bay leaf

First, make the onion jam. Heat the olive oil in a medium saucepan, then add the onions and bay leaf and cook gently until soft. Keep cooking them over low heat for about an hour, or until they slowly start turning golden brown and the natural sugars start to caramelize. At this point you can chill the jam and keep it in the fridge (you could make a double batch and save half for future use).

Cook the potatoes in a saucepan of salted water for approximately 20 minutes. When ready, strain and let cool. Cut each one in half.

Preheat your oven to 350°F.

Put the chorizo, potatoes, and a drizzle of olive oil into an ovenproof skillet and place in the oven for 10 minutes. Add the peperonata and onion jam and give it a stir. Return the pan to the oven for a further 10 minutes. Next, crack the eggs on top and cover with the cheese. Return the pan to the oven until the cheese is melted and the white of the egg is cooked, but the yolk is still runny—approximately 5 to 10 minutes, depending on how you like your eggs. Remove from the oven and season with salt and pepper. The egg will continue to cook, so serve immediately.

We serve fresh fish from Cornwall & Scotland. Our meats are from the RHUG Estate, North Wales...

www.facebook.com/duckandwaffle

Meatballs are one of the best comfort foods around. This recipe is one of my favorites—the ricotta gets moved around the dish as you eat, so the sauce becomes slightly enriched and creamy. Once you master meatballs, you'll have great fun playing with flavor combinations, changing the meats and spices, the sauces, and the starch. Personally, I like a good scoop of mashed potatoes with mine, but bread or pasta also work just fine. You can buy ricotta if you don't have time to make it.

# Meatballs with Fennel and Ricotta

**Serves:** 4
**Preparation time:** 1 hour
**Cooking time:** 30 minutes

1 stick butter, divided

1 cup fresh bread crumbs

olive oil

1 head of fennel, sliced paper-thin on a mandoline slicer

2 tablespoons Onion Jam (see page 36)

2 cups Chicken Stock (see page 216)

sea salt and freshly ground black pepper

½ cup grated Parmesan cheese

2 tablespoons pine nuts, toasted

**For the ricotta**

4¼ pints whole milk

a pinch of sea salt

juice of 2 lemons

**For the meatballs**

1 pound 2 ounces ground pork

3½ ounces finocchiona salami, finely diced or ground

1 cup fresh bread crumbs

1 egg

a pinch of fennel seeds

1 sprig of fresh rosemary, finely chopped

1 sprig of fresh oregano, finely chopped

First, make the ricotta. Heat the milk until just below boiling, then add the salt and the lemon juice and let stand, undisturbed, for 10 minutes. After this time, the milk should have curdled. Strain through a muslin cloth and let stand for a further 30 minutes. You can use it at this stage, or wrap it in the cloth and hang it in your fridge, above a bowl, for a drier ricotta.

Melt ½ stick of the butter in a skillet over medium heat and add the bread crumbs. Toast until golden brown, stirring often. If they start to color too quickly, lower the heat. Set aside and let cool.

To make the meatballs, combine all the ingredients together and mix well. Roll into golfball-size balls.

Preheat your oven to 350°F.

Heat a drizzle of olive oil in a skillet, then add the meatballs and brown them all over to seal. Put them into a baking dish.

Put the shaved fennel into the same skillet with 1 tablespoon olive oil and cook gently for approximately 10 minutes. Add the onion jam and the chicken stock, bring to a boil, then reduce the heat and simmer until reduced by three-quarters. Add the remaining butter and swirl it around so that it emulsifies and combines into a sauce, then season with salt and pepper. Pour the mixture over the meatballs.

Place in the oven for 10 minutes, then remove, sprinkle with the Parmesan, and spoon over a couple of tablespoons of ricotta. Put back into the oven for a further 5 minutes, or until the Parmesan has browned. Take out, scatter evenly with the reserved browned bread crumbs and pine nuts, and serve immediately.

**Makes:** 4

**Preparation time:** 30 minutes

**Cooking time:** 10 to 20 minutes, depending on how you want your burgers cooked

### For the burger mix

1 onion, minced

2 tablespoons vegetable oil

sea salt and freshly ground black pepper

10½ ounces short loin beef, ground

10½ ounces chuck steak, ground

1 dill pickle, minced

2 cloves of Confit Garlic (see page 217)

1 tablespoon Dijon mustard

2 splashes of Tabasco

### For the special sauce

2 tablespoons Mayonnaise (see page 217)

1 tablespoon tomato ketchup

1 dill pickle, minced

1 shallot, minced

1 teaspoon English mustard

2 sprigs of fresh dill, finely chopped

1 tablespoon Sriracha hot sauce

### To assemble

4 slices Gruyère cheese

4 brioche buns

4 tablespoons Onion Jam (see page 36)

8 Little Gem leaves

Leo Sayer—all dayer. Modern London cockney rhyming slang. Zeren Wilson, of Bitten & Written, once did an all-nighter when we first opened, and it was when he said he was "on a Leo" that the idea struck me. We wanted to create a burger that satisfied everyone's needs over a 24-hour period, and this is what we came up with. Needless to say, upon request, eggs, bacon, avocado, hash browns, and mushrooms have all been added (once all together in a single burger), so I'll leave the "extras" to you.

# Leo Sayer Burger

For the burger, first cook the onion gently in the oil for a few minutes without coloring. Add the cooked onion to a large bowl, season with salt and pepper, combine with all the other burger ingredients, and work together well to combine. Divide into 4 and shape into patties.

For the special sauce, mix all the ingredients together in a bowl.

Cook the burgers on a ridged grill pan or, even better, on a barbecue, for 3 minutes on each side for medium rare, 4 minutes for medium, and 6 to 8 minutes for well done.

Place the cheese on top and melt under a hot broiler for 1 minute, then build up your buns with the special sauce, onion jam, Little Gem leaves, and whatever else takes your fancy.

There is no recipe as such for this; everyone has different "needs" in their time of pain. The idea came from my time in Miami, when, on my second-to-last day, we all went out and got a little crazy, and to say I was feeling it the next day would be the understatement of the year. Eric, one of the managers, demanded I ate one of his hangover pizzas, and wouldn't take no for an answer. Knowing Eric well, most of the chefs knew exactly what it consisted of, and, after a good 10 minutes of pushing through, my hangover was cured. Below is my medicine; yours will be different, no doubt.

# Hangover Pizza

**Serves:** 1

**Preparation time:** 1½ hours

**Cooking time:** 12 minutes (maybe longer if you add more ingredients…)

**For the dough**

3¼ cups strong white flour

¾ cup semolina flour

2 teaspoons sea salt

¼ ounce fresh yeast or 1 sachet of fast-acting instant yeast

1¼ cups lukewarm water

3 tablespoons olive oil

2 tablespoons passata (thick tomato purée)

4 strips of bacon, cooked

a small handful of shredded Cheddar cheese

½ a ball of mozzarella cheese, torn into quarters

3 splashes of hot sauce

1 tablespoon Peperonata (see page 59)

1 tablespoon Onion Jam (see page 36)

1 egg

another handful of shredded Cheddar

more bacon

more cheese

This is so wrong, my wife would kill me. But anyway, the cure begins…

To make the dough, sift the flours together and add the salt. Mix the yeast, water, and oil together in a bowl. Make a well in the flour, and add the yeast liquid. Gradually work the flour and liquid together to form a dough. Continue to knead for 10 minutes, or until the dough is smooth and elastic. Set it aside to rest for 1 hour, or until doubled in size.

Preheat your oven to as hot as it will go and line a sturdy cookie sheet with oiled nonstick parchment paper.

On a floured surface, give the dough a quick knead to knock the air out of it. Roll the dough out nice and thin, aiming for the thickness of a dime, give or take, and place it on the prepared cookie sheet.

Build up the toppings creating cheesy layers, and leaving the egg until last. If loading lots of ingredients, you may want to precook your crust so it doesn't get soggy. Make sure you create a small dip in the center so the egg doesn't roll out.

Bake for approximately 10 to 12 minutes, or until the dough is cooked and crisp. Note that this varies from oven to oven, so keep a close eye on it.

Another comfort food idea, this is one traditionally made with beef. You can omit the lamb's breast if you don't have time to cure and confit—it's just there for a nice crunch, which can also be achieved by crumbling some salted potato chips on top (sounds strange, but it works).

# Smoky Mutton Sloppy Joe with Crispy Lamb's Breast

**Makes:** 6
**Preparation time:** 1 day
**Cooking time:** 4½ hours

### For the lamb

3½-ounce piece of lamb's breast

3½ ounces Standard Cure (see page 218)

1 cup duck fat

vegetable oil, for frying

all-purpose flour, for dusting

sea salt and freshly ground black pepper

### For the sloppy Joe mix

1 pound 2 ounces ground mutton

2 onions, minced

2 garlic cloves, minced

4 chipotles en adobo from a jar, mashed to a rough paste

2 teaspoons harissa

2 sprigs of fresh rosemary

4 bay leaves

2½ tablespoons tomato paste

¾ cup tomato ketchup

¼ cup Worcestershire sauce

¼ cup soy sauce

### To assemble

6 brioche hot dog buns

fresh cilantro leaves, to garnish

The day before, sprinkle the lamb's breast all over with the cure. Put it into a container with a lid and leave in the fridge overnight.

The next day, preheat your oven to 265°F. Take out the lamb's breast and brush off all of the cure. Place the lamb in a baking dish, add the duck fat to cover, and confit for approximately 3 hours, or until the meat is tender and gives easily when pushed with a spoon. Let cool in the fat. When cool enough to handle, pull the meat into strands with your fingers, then store in the fridge.

To make the sloppy Joe mix, put the ground mutton into a skillet over medium heat, and discard any fat as it melts. Add the onions and garlic and continue to cook for a further 10 minutes, or until the onions are soft. Add the remaining sloppy Joe ingredients and cook over low heat for approximately 1 hour, as you would any ragout.

Heat the oil to 350°F in a deep-fat fryer or in a deep heavy saucepan. Dust a handful of the lamb's breast with flour and fry for 2 to 3 minutes, or until crisp. Place on paper towels to dry, and season with salt and pepper.

Flash the brioche buns in a warm oven or toast them lightly, and serve the sloppy Joe mixture in the buns, the same way as you would a hot dog. Garnish with the crispy lamb breast and the cilantro leaves.

Extreme gluttony alert! Another 4 A.M. before-you-go-to-sleep or 10 A.M. I-need-some-love dish. As always, feel free to add one of the magical three: bacon, more cheese, or hot sauce.

# Grilled Cheese with Ox Cheek and Pickled Fennel

**Serves:** 2

**Preparation time:** 20 minutes (if you have ox cheek braised already), plus pickling time

**Cooking time:** 20 to 25 minutes

4 slices of sourdough bread

3½ ounces Braised Ox Cheek (see page 102)

4 slices Taleggio cheese, cut to the same size as your bread

scant ½ stick unsalted butter, divided

8 pieces of Pickled Fennel (see below)

2 tablespoons Hollandaise (see page 34)

**For the pickled fennel**

1 head of fennel

1¼ cups Pickling Liquid (see page 216)

Slice the fennel paper-thin and add it to a bowl. Pour the pickling liquid over it to cover and let stand for at least 3 hours.

Take 2 slices of bread and divide the ox cheek between them. Add 2 slices of cheese to each. Close the sandwich with the other 2 slices of bread.

Heat an ovenproof skillet and preheat your oven to 350°F.

Add half the butter to the skillet. When it's foaming, add the sandwiches and cook until golden brown. Carefully turn them over and add the other half of the butter. Place in the oven until the cheese is melted, the ox cheek is hot and the bread is golden brown on the bottom. This should take around 10 minutes.

Remove from the oven and place each sandwich on a plate. Open them up and add 4 pieces of the pickled fennel and a tablespoon of hollandaise to each one. Close up the sandwiches and eat immediately.

SMALL PLATES

Using granola in a savory salad adds a different texture and dimension. Try using different fruits and nuts to suit your fancy. Use Amalfi lemons if you can get them, because they are, simply put, the best lemons in the world. If you can't find Amalfi lemons, any unwaxed lemon will do. Another good ingredient to have in your cupboard is balsamic glaze; at the restaurant we reduce aged balsamic vinegar to create a beautiful glaze that's both sweet and acidic, but this can be tricky to get right, and now you can buy it in most supermarkets to save you the stress. If you would like to try making your own, see page 217.

# Smoked Ricotta with Granola and Candied Lemon

**Serves:** 4

**Preparation time:** 10 minutes (if you have the candied lemon, granola, and balsamic glaze ready; 2 hours, plus drying time if not)

**Assembly time:** 20 minutes

10 fresh sage leaves

vegetable oil, for frying

3 cups watercress

1¼ cups Granola (see page 218)

3½ ounces smoked ricotta (or ricotta salata if you can't find smoked ricotta), shaved with a peeler

2 tablespoons Sherry Dressing (see page 216)

2 teaspoons Balsamic Glaze (see page 217)

2 teaspoons honey

3 teaspoons of Candied Lemon (see below)

**For the candied lemon**

2 Amalfi lemons

2 pints water, divided

½ cup superfine sugar

To make the candied lemon, peel the rind from the lemons and trim off any white pith. Slice the rind into matchstick-size pieces. Bring 1¼ cups of the water to a boil in a saucepan. Add the lemon rind, and let stand for 10 seconds. Remove from the water and place in iced water to stop the cooking process. Repeat this process three times. This removes any bitterness from the lemon rind.

Put the sugar into a saucepan with the remaining scant ½ cup of water and stir to dissolve. Bring to a boil, then add the blanched lemon rind and simmer for 5 minutes. Remove and spread out on a cookie sheet lined with nonstick parchment paper. Let dry for a few hours, or until crisp.

Meanwhile, fry the sage leaves in hot oil for 10 seconds, or until crisp, and drain on paper towels.

To make the salad, put the watercress, granola, and ricotta into a bowl and dress with the sherry dressing. Arrange with plenty of height on a serving plate or in a bowl. Drizzle over the balsamic and honey, then scatter with the sage leaves and the candied lemon.

This is one of our most popular dishes at the restaurant; as the fresh goat curd sits on the hot beets, fresh from our brick oven, it slowly melts to make an unctuous creamy sauce so, as you eat it, the dish is slowly changing for the better. If you can get heirloom beets, using all the different varieties, it's great, because the variety of color really enhances the presentation.

# Roasted Beets with Goat Curd, Honeycomb, and Watercress

Serves: 6

**Preparation time:** 20 minutes (providing the honeycomb is already made)

**Cooking time:** 2 hours

2¼ pounds uncooked beets

1 sprig of fresh thyme

1 sprig of fresh rosemary

4 garlic cloves

2 tablespoons olive oil

sea salt and freshly ground black pepper

1 tablespoon Confit Shallots (see page 217)

scant ½ cup Sherry Dressing (see page 216)

7 ounces goat curd

2½ ounces Honeycomb (see page 219)

3 cups watercress

Preheat your oven to 320°F.

Wash the beets and pierce each one two or three times with a knife. Line a roasting pan with foil, put the beets in, add the thyme, rosemary, and garlic and cover with more foil. Place in the oven and roast for about 1½ hours, or until a knife goes into the beets easily. Remove the foil and let the beets cool, then peel and discard the skin, along with the herbs and garlic (wearing disposable gloves to stop your fingers from turning pink). This can be done up to 2 days in advance.

Preheat your oven to 350°F.

Arrange the beets in a baking dish. If they are quite big, you can cut them into smaller pieces (1 to 2 inches works best). Add the olive oil and make sure all the pieces are coated, then season with salt and pepper.

Place in the oven for 10 minutes, then remove and add the confit shallots and half the sherry dressing. Give them a little stir, then spoon on the curd in tablespoon-size dollops, and scatter with pieces of honeycomb. Garnish with the watercress, dressed with the rest of the sherry dressing.

I'm not sure what it is about charred broccoli and Caesar dressing, but it's a great combination that I come back to time and time again. It makes an interesting side for roast chicken, and it's also a good dish in itself.

# Grilled Sprouting Broccoli with Caesar Dressing

**Serves:** 4

**Preparation time:** 15 minutes

**Cooking time:** 30 minutes

1 pound 5 ounces sprouting broccoli

sea salt

2 tablespoons olive oil

½ a lemon

¼ cup sliced almonds, toasted

**For the Caesar dressing**

¼ cup Mayonnaise (see page 217)

2 brown anchovy fillets, finely chopped

2 cloves of Confit Garlic (see page 217), peeled and ground to a paste

¼ cup grated Parmesan cheese

To make the Caesar dressing, blend all the ingredients together and set aside.

Blanch the broccoli in salted boiling water for about a minute. Refresh in iced water and drain once cold.

Heat a ridged grill pan over high heat (or you can use a barbecue). Put the broccoli into a mixing bowl and toss with the olive oil until well coated, then place on the grill pan (depending on the size of your pan you may need to cook the broccoli in batches). Don't worry if it gets dark marks—they really add to the flavor.

When the broccoli is evenly colored, place it in a mixing bowl. Add a squeeze of lemon and some sea salt. Pour the Caesar dressing onto the broccoli and toss. Transfer to serving plates and finish each one with a sprinkling of toasted almonds.

These work well on a barbecue, and they look fun, too. Adjust the spices to suit your fancy.

# Charred Corn on the Cob with Jerk Spices and Coconut

**Makes:** 6

**Preparation time:** 20 minutes

**Cooking time:** 40 minutes

6 corn on the cob

sea salt

1 teaspoon prepared jerk spice, toasted

1 chipotle en adobo from a jar

3 sprigs of fresh cilantro, chopped

3 tablespoons Mayonnaise (see page 217)

1¼ cups desiccated shredded coconut, toasted

Place the corn in a large saucepan, add a pinch of salt, and cover with cold water. Bring to a boil, then lower the heat and simmer for 15 minutes.

Maintain medium heat on your barbecue, or heat a ridged grill pan. Drain the corn, then place it directly on the barbecue or grill pan on the stove over medium heat. Don't be scared if it starts to get dark marks—they give it a great flavor. When the corn is evenly colored, take it off the heat and place it on a plate or cutting board.

Mix the toasted jerk spice, chipotle chile, and cilantro into the mayo. Spread the mayo all over the corn cobs, until they are coated evenly, and finally roll each one in the toasted coconut. Serve immediately.

This is a great recipe to keep up your sleeve. It's amazing served simply with bread, in our pearl barley recipe (see page 23), or with fresh burrata or mozzarella. The tangy flavor goes with pretty much anything, and it lasts a while, too. I always have a jar of this at home. Try adding freshly chopped basil just before using.

# Peperonata

**Makes:** 2¼ pounds
**Preparation time:** 30 minutes
**Cooking time:** 1 to 1½ hours

scant ½ cup olive oil

6 red bell peppers, seeded and sliced ¼ inch thick

2 red onions, finely sliced

2 garlic cloves, minced

sea salt and freshly ground black pepper

10 plum tomatoes, seeded and sliced

1 bay leaf

2 sprigs of fresh thyme

2 tablespoons dark brown sugar

scant ½ cup red wine vinegar

finely grated zest of 1 lemon

Heat the oil in a large saucepan, then add the peppers, onions, and garlic and cook gently for 15 to 20 minutes without coloring. Season with salt and pepper, then add the rest of the ingredients and continue to cook until the mixture has a nice semi-thick sauce consistency. Keep an eye on it and stir it often, to make sure it doesn't burn.

Remove and discard the bay leaf and thyme, and store in a sterilized jar in the fridge until you need it. This will keep for up to 1 month.

Artichokes are one of my favorite vegetables, and this is one that works well on the barbecue, too. Try using a different cheese, or swapping the bacon for chorizo or n'duja.

# Roasted Artichokes with Caerphilly Crumble

**Serves:** 4

**Preparation time:** 1 hour

**Cooking time:** 45 minutes

2 globe artichokes

1 lemon

4 strips of smoked bacon, cut into ½-inch pieces

1 tablespoon Confit Shallots (see page 217)

2 cloves of Confit Garlic (see page 217)

4 slices of white bread, crusts removed, cut into ½-inch cubes

3½ ounces Caerphilly cheese, crumbled

1 sprig of fresh parsley, chopped

1 leaf of fresh chives, chopped

olive oil

freshly ground black pepper

You will also need a steamer

Set up a steamer ready for the artichokes.

Trim the end of each artichoke, about 1 inch down (not the stalk end, the bulbous end). Cut the lemon in half and rub the area of artichoke you cut to prevent it from going brown, then continue to do so every time you make a cut. Trim the outside leaves to make them square, not pointy. Peel the stem of each artichoke with a peeler or a knife, then cut about 2 inches from the artichoke heart and discard. Cut the artichokes in half and then, with a spoon, scoop out the central feathery part and the smallest leaves.

Put the artichokes into the steamer, cut-side up, and steam for 20 minutes.

To make the stuffing, cook the bacon in a skillet until the fat comes out, then add the confit shallots and confit garlic. Add the bread cubes—the idea is that the bread absorbs the fat, which essentially contains the flavor. Let the bread take on a little color at this stage, too. Transfer the contents of the pan to a mixing bowl and add the cheese and herbs.

Preheat your oven to 350°F.

Put 2 tablespoons of the stuffing mix into the center of each artichoke, where you removed the inner leaves. Drizzle with olive oil and a grinding of black pepper. Place in the oven (or on the barbecue) for about 10 to 12 minutes, or until nicely browned.

New season's asparagus, crispy meat, and a runny egg are a combination to die for. Here, we have taken out the more familiar pancetta or Serrano ham, and use chicken skin instead. And rather than use a poached egg, we slowly confit an egg yolk in olive oil, which really brings the dish together. Try adding wild mushrooms to the foaming butter with the asparagus when in season—morels would be perfect.

# Asparagus with Crispy Chicken Skin and Confit Egg Yolk

**Serves:** 4

**Preparation time:** 20 minutes

**Cooking time:** 2 hours

4¼ ounces chicken skin (approximately 4 breasts' or legs' worth)

sea salt and freshly ground black pepper

2 bunches of asparagus

4 egg yolks

olive oil, to cover

1½ tablespoons butter

1 handful of pea shoots

1 teaspoon Sherry Dressing (see page 216)

The chicken skin and the asparagus can be prepared in advance.

Preheat your oven to 350°F.

Line a cookie sheet with nonstick parchment paper and spread the pieces of skin out so they are completely flat. Season with salt, then cover with another sheet of parchment paper. If you have another cookie sheet, place it on top so the pieces of skin stay flat and thin. If not, don't worry; they will just curl up a bit. Place in the oven for about 20 minutes (each oven is different, though, so check every 5 minutes to make sure the skin is not burning). You're looking for a crisp skin that's golden brown. Remove from the oven and transfer to a rack to cool.

Prepare your asparagus by removing the little ears on the stalks (some people like to peel it with a peeler, but I think this gives too much waste) and cutting about 2 inches from the base (where it begins to be woody). Blanch the asparagus in salted boiling water for about 30 seconds, then refresh in iced water and drain.

To confit the egg yolks, preheat your oven to 150°F, or as low as possible, an hour before serving. Separate the eggs, making sure all the white and membrane is removed, then place the yolks in a baking dish. Add enough olive oil to cover them completely. Place in the oven for 40 minutes, or longer if you like a firmer yolk.

Heat a large skillet and add the butter. When it starts to foam, add the asparagus and let them color a little, but no more than 3 minutes.

To serve, arrange your asparagus on a plate with a confit egg yolk in the center and shards of crispy chicken skin next to it. Season with a little salt and pepper and finish with the pea shoots, and drizzle all over with the sherry dressing.

This is one of my favorite spring recipes, bursting with flavor and color; it really gets you in the mood for summer. The flavor of the concentrated tomatoes does make a difference, but if you don't have time to make them, try using half fresh and half sun-dried.

# Grilled Asparagus with Pink Grapefruit Sauce Vierge

**Serves:** 6
**Preparation time:** 1 day
**Cooking time:** 5 minutes

20 cherry tomatoes

sea salt and freshly ground black pepper

scant ½ cup olive oil

1 pink grapefruit

20 fresh basil leaves, divided

2 tablespoons Confit Shallots (see page 217)

1 clove of Confit Garlic (see page 217)

1 tablespoon sherry vinegar

3 bunches of asparagus

3 tablespoons Balsamic Glaze (see page 217)

Preheat your oven to its lowest setting.

Cut each tomato in half and put them, cut-side up, on a cookie sheet lined with nonstick parchment paper. Season with salt, pepper, and a drizzle of olive oil and put into the oven on the lowest setting for a couple of hours, or until dried. You can turn the oven off and let the tomatoes dry out in the oven overnight; the slower you dry them, the better.

When the tomatoes are dried, roughly chop them into ¼-inch pieces and add to a small mixing bowl. Segment the grapefruit and chop into similar-size pieces. Add the grapefruit to the tomatoes, then add the scant ½ cup olive oil, 12 of the basil leaves, the confit shallots, garlic, and sherry vinegar and stir with a spoon. Set aside while you start the asparagus.

Prepare your asparagus by removing the little ears from the stalks (some people like to peel with a peeler, but I think this gives too much waste) and cutting about 2 inches from the base (where it begins to be woody). Blanch in salted boiling water for about 30 seconds, then refresh in iced water and drain.

Heat a ridged grill pan over high heat. Lightly oil and season your asparagus. Grill for a couple of minutes, or until you have nice char lines, rotating the spears so they are colored and cooked all over.

Arrange the asparagus on plates with the sauce spooned around, and finish with the rest of the basil leaves. A little of that magical balsamic glaze drizzled over at this stage really lifts the dish.

Piedmont's answer to fondue, bagna cauda is a northern Italian classic. Normally used for dipping vegetables, I like to pair it with roasted cauliflower and finish with tangy pickled walnuts to cut the richness. Traditionally it's quite pungent in the garlic department, but you can add or subtract, as you like (I use confit garlic to soften it a little).

# Roasted Cauliflower with Bagna Cauda and Pickled Walnuts

**Serves:** 4

**Preparation time:** 10 minutes

**Cooking time:** 25 minutes

sea salt

1 large cauliflower, cut into florets

½ cup + 2 tablespoons olive oil, divided, the best you can get

1 sprig of fresh rosemary

4 cloves of Confit Garlic (see page 217)

10 brown anchovy fillets

1 stick unsalted butter, cut into ¾-inch cubes

8 pickled walnuts (best to buy them ready-pickled in a jar)

**To garnish**

2 handfuls of watercress

1 tablespoon Sherry Dressing (see page 216)

Bring a saucepan of salted water to a boil, then add your cauliflower and blanch for 1 minute. Refresh in iced water, then drain and dry.

Preheat your oven to 320°F. Place the cauliflower florets in a roasting pan and lightly drizzle with 2 tablespoons of the olive oil. Add the rosemary and place in the oven for about 25 minutes, or until lightly browned.

In the meantime, make the bagna cauda. Put the garlic, anchovies, and the remaining ½ cup of olive oil into a saucepan and whisk together over medium heat. Add the butter, 5 to 6 cubes at a time, and whisk continuously so the mixture emulsifies and becomes creamy.

When the cauliflower is ready, remove from the oven and divide between your serving plates. Drizzle the bagna cauda over and around the cauliflower, and place 2 pickled walnuts (break them into pieces using your fingers), on top. Garnish with the watercress, dressed with the sherry dressing.

The vegetables are the stars of the show here, with the lardo more of a middle man to bring all the flavors together. If you have a farm stand nearby, go and see them, as they will have the best produce for this. If you can't get lardo, try using Parma ham instead. It has a much lower fat content, so you may need to add a touch of olive oil, but it will give a nice pork flavor.

# Slow-roasted Heirloom Carrots with Lardo, Peas, and Mint

**Serves:** 4

**Preparation time:** 20 minutes

**Cooking time:** 20 minutes

8 heirloom carrots, about 6 inches long

sea salt and freshly ground black pepper

4 slices of lardo, about 12 x 2½ inches, ¹/₁₆-inch thick

1 tablespoon Confit Shallots (see page 217)

2 cloves of Confit Garlic (see page 217)

1 cup freshly shelled peas (or frozen, if not in season), blanched and refreshed

scant 1 cup Chicken Stock (see page 216)

1 tablespoon olive oil

3 tablespoons butter, divided

8 fresh mint leaves

Cut the green stems off the carrots, but feel free to leave a little of them on if you like, for presentation. Peel and halve the carrots lengthwise, then blanch in salted boiling water for about 5 minutes, depending on size (a knife should go through with a little pressure), then refresh in iced water.

Put a sauté pan over medium heat. Add the lardo and let it melt so that it releases its fat. Add the confit shallots and garlic, season with salt and pepper, then add the peas and give everything a good stir. Now add the chicken stock and turn up the heat so it reduces rapidly.

To serve, put another sauté pan over medium heat and add the olive oil. Add the carrots and let them lightly brown, turning them as they color. When almost done, add half of the butter and allow it to foam and give the carrots a nutty flavor.

When the chicken stock has reduced by three-quarters, add the remaining butter, lower the heat, and give it a good stir to emulsify and enrich the ragout. Remove any lardo that hasn't melted and discard. Finely chop the mint and stir into the ragout. Arrange the carrots on a warm serving plate and spoon the ragout over and around.

This raw dish has been on the menu at the restaurant since day one, and people seem to love it. Anything raw, or "crudo," needs to have three basic elements—salt, oil, and acidity. Then you can add textures, spices, or herbs as you wish. This is great for a chef, because as long as you have each element in the dish, you can be as creative as you like. For example, instead of seasoning with salt, we use a salt brick as a plate, so the fish absorbs the seasoning. Salt can also come in the form of capers or samphire, and acidity with lime or sherry vinegar, and so on.

# Tuna with Watermelon, Balsamic, and Basil

**Serves:** 4

**Preparation time:** 10 minutes (or prepare the watermelon the day before)

**Cooking time:** 5 minutes

¼ cup superfine sugar

3 tablespoons water

1 red chile (seeds removed if you don't want too much of a kick), coarsely chopped

⅔ cup of ½-inch cubes of watermelon

1 piece of fresh tuna, approximately 7 ounces, or the size of a chocolate bar. (If you can't get it in the shape of a bar, you can buy a tuna steak and cut it into cubes instead—see method)

Balsamic Glaze (see page 217)

fresh basil leaves

sea salt

The watermelon gets better with time, so while you can make and eat this right away, if you are able to prepare the watermelon the day before, the flavor becomes much deeper. Put the sugar and water into a saucepan and bring to a boil. Remove from the heat and add the chile. Let cool. When cold, add the watermelon cubes. These can now be used immediately or can be left in the fridge to marinate until the next day.

Slice the tuna ⅛ inch thick and spread out on a plate. Put a cube of watermelon on top of each slice. Add a drizzle of balsamic glaze and some leaves of basil, cut into ½-inch pieces, to each one. Finish with sea salt and serve immediately.

If using a tuna steak, cut the tuna into ½-inch dice and place in a mixing bowl. Add 1 teaspoon of watermelon cubes per 1 tablespoon of tuna. Add the basil, season, and stir. Divide between serving plates and finish with a drizzle of balsamic glaze.

**Serves:** 4

**Preparation time:** 20 minutes

**Cooking time:** 1 hour

**For the lobster cream sauce**

1 lobster carcass

3 tablespoons olive oil

2 shallots, chopped

2 garlic cloves, crushed

1 stalk of celery,
cut into ½-inch pieces

1 sprig of fresh thyme

1 bay leaf

1 tablespoon tomato paste

1 glass of white wine

scant 1 cup Chicken Stock
(see page 216), or vegetable stock

2 cups heavy cream, or enough
to cover

sea salt and freshly ground
black pepper

**For the fishballs**

1 pound 2 ounces pollock, or any
other white fish, such as haddock,
cod, or hake, skinned and cut into
1-inch pieces

2 egg whites

1 sprig of fresh tarragon

1 sprig of fresh parsley

1 leaf of fresh chives

grated zest of 1 lemon

**To finish**

1 stick butter

1⅔ cups fresh bread crumbs

1 cup grated Parmesan cheese

This dish came about when we had grilled lobster on the menu, and were using perfect squares of pollock for another dish. To prevent any waste, we made a cream sauce from the lobster shells, and used the pollock trimmings to make fishballs. It's so popular now that we are buying the fish and lobster specifically for this; it's real comfort food and goes well with our homemade breads. The sauce is also great with pasta, or as a base for a fish pie.

# Cornish Pollock Fishballs with Lobster Cream and Parmesan

First, make the sauce. Take the lobster carcass and, using scissors, break it into 5 or 6 pieces. Put the olive oil into a large saucepan over medium heat and, when hot, add the pieces of lobster shell. Cook for about 8 minutes, or until they dry out and start to color a little.

Add the shallots, garlic, celery, thyme, and bay leaf and continue to cook for a further 5 minutes. Add the tomato paste, stir well, and continue to cook over medium heat, without coloring, for 5 minutes. Add the wine and simmer until reduced by three-quarters, then add the stock and reduce by three-quarters again. Add the cream, reduce the heat, and let simmer for 30 minutes. Strain through a sieve, and correct the seasoning.

Next, make the fishballs. Put the fish and egg whites into a blender and blend until smooth. Transfer the mixture to a bowl and add the herbs and lemon zest. Season with salt and pepper. Roll into golfball-size balls and refrigerate until you are ready to cook.

Melt the butter in a skillet over medium heat and add the bread crumbs. Toast until golden brown, stirring often. If they start to color too quickly, reduce the heat. Let cool.

Preheat your oven to 350°F. Put the fishballs into an earthenware baking dish, evenly spaced out, and pour the sauce over them. Place in the oven for about 12 minutes, then take out, sprinkle evenly with the Parmesan, and return to the oven for a further 5 minutes.

Just before serving, sprinkle with 3 to 4 tablespoons of the browned bread crumbs.

Playing with the three basic components of "crudo," or raw, dishes (salt, oil, and acidity), we use pickled shimeji mushrooms and lime for acidity, blueberry and truffle to give a sweet earthiness, and finish with arugula leaves or winter cress for a nice peppery punch. The colors are striking, and it tastes pretty good, too.

# Halibut Tartare with Blueberries and Pickled Mushrooms

**Serves:** 4

**Preparation time:** 3 hours, 20 minutes

**Cooking time:** 10 minutes

16 shimeji mushrooms, or 4 shiitake if you can't find shimeji

Pickling Liquid, enough to cover (see page 216)

1⅓ cups blueberries

juice of ½ a lemon

1 pound 2 ounces fresh halibut, skinned

a squeeze of lime juice

sea salt

winter cress, to garnish (arugula leaves are fine, too)

1 teaspoon truffle oil

4 slices of sourdough bread, toasted

First, pickle the mushrooms. This can be done well in advance, as the longer you can let them pickle, the better. You need 16 mushrooms for this recipe, but you can pickle them in larger numbers—they will keep for up to 1 month. Bring the pickling liquid to a boil. Have your mushrooms ready in a sterilized jar or jars, then pour the hot pickling liquid over them and seal. Let stand for at least 3 hours before using.

To make the blueberry coulis, put the blueberries into a small saucepan with the lemon juice, bring to a boil, then lower the heat and simmer until reduced to a thick compote. Scrape through a fine sieve, then let cool. It will taste very sharp, but that's fine—it's all part of the plan.

When ready to serve, slice the halibut into ¼-inch cubes and place them in a chilled mixing bowl. Add 3 teaspoons of the blueberry coulis, a squeeze of lime, and a pinch of sea salt. Give it a good stir, and place on a serving plate. Garnish with the pickled shimeji, some winter cress or arugula leaves, and drizzle with truffle oil. Serve with warm toast on the side.

I love how well octopus and chorizo go together, and with salty capers and sharp lemon segments, this dish has it all. After it had been on the menu for about a year, we decided to add some new potatoes—they caramelize in the oils from the chorizo and really help the balance of the dish. If octopus is too hard to find, try using squid. You won't need to precook it, just add it raw with the chorizo in the final step.

# Roasted Octopus with Chorizo, Potato, and Caper Berries

**Serves:** 4

**Preparation time:** 1 hour

**Cooking time:** about 1 hour

1 daikon radish

1 octopus, approximately 2¼ pounds, cleaned (ask your fish dealer to remove the head)

1 onion

2 stalks of celery

2 carrots

1 bay leaf

1 sprig of fresh thyme

10 black peppercorns

scant 1 cup red wine

2 tablespoons olive oil

10 new potatoes, cooked and halved

9 ounces cooked smoked chorizo sausage, casing removed, cut into ½-inch dice

2 tablespoons Confit Shallots (see page 217)

1 lemon, segmented

1 sprig of fresh parsley, finely chopped

sea salt and freshly ground black pepper

2 pinches of caper berries, deep-fried for 30 seconds until crisp, to garnish

To prepare the octopus, we do something a little different from usual to tenderize it. First, cut the daikon radish in half and rub the cut ends all over the octopus. The enzymes in the daikon help to tenderize the octopus, which can be incredibly tough. Then we give it a massage—sounds crazy, I know. Basically, give a little pull at 1-inch intervals all the way down each tentacle.

Place your rubbed and massaged octopus in a large saucepan, and add the onion, celery, carrots, herbs, and peppercorns. Pour in the wine and enough cold water to cover and slowly bring to a boil. Reduce the heat and simmer for about 45 to 60 minutes, or until the octopus is tender. Let it cool in the stock, then transfer to a cutting board, taking care as the skin is delicate and can come away. Cut into 1-inch pieces, discarding the vegetables.

When ready to serve, heat the olive oil in a skillet. Add the potatoes and the pieces of octopus and lightly brown. Next add the chorizo and cook until the fats are released. Sauté together for 2 to 3 minutes, then add the confit shallots, lemon segments, and parsley. Give everything a good stir to let the ingredients get to know one another for a few minutes, then plate up, seasoning with salt and pepper and garnishing with the crispy capers.

I love oysters whether straight up or cooked. There are some great classic ways of cooking oysters in every cuisine. This dish was inspired by a conversation with one of our regulars. While catching up and discussing the menu, I mentioned how good I thought our Irish oysters were. On hearing that they only ate cooked oysters, and knowing the flavors they liked, I played around with some ideas and this ended up on the menu.

# Broiled Oysters with Spicy Bacon Butter

**Serves:** 2 to 3
**Preparation time:** 10 minutes
**Cooking time:** 10 minutes

6 of the best, freshest oysters you can find

3 strips smoked bacon, or pancetta if you can find it, cut into ⅛-inch lardons

½ stick butter

1 tablespoon Confit Shallots (see page 217)

a few splashes of Tabasco

½ a lemon

1 sprig of fresh parsley, finely chopped

2 tablespoons bread crumbs

First, open your oysters carefully and place them on a broiler rack. If you're unsure how to open them, it's best to look at a video on the internet—describing how to do it here could be tricky and I'd hate you to waste an oyster! Preheat your broiler to a medium-hot temperature.

To make the butter, place a skillet over medium heat. Add the bacon and cook for a few minutes, or until it's a little crisp and brown. Next, add the butter and wait for it to begin to foam. Add the shallots and give a good stir. Let the butter continue to cook until almost nutty brown, then add a few splashes of Tabasco, to taste. Soon after this the butter will become a nutty brown, so take it off the heat and squeeze the lemon over it. It will spatter a little, so be careful.

Finish the sauce with the chopped parsley, then spoon 1 tablespoon onto each oyster. Sprinkle each one with bread crumbs and place under the broiler for 1 to 2 minutes.

Be careful when eating, as the oyster shell can be quite warm.

This is what we call a one-pot wonder—it's so easy to make, and is tasty as hell. In my opinion, this dish represents what cooking and eating are all about: great produce, cooked simply, and eaten with your sleeves rolled up and a couple of slices of bread to mop up the juices. If you are ever in London, make the trip to Billingsgate Market—it's well worth the 4 A.M. start, and the breakfast in the café at the end is pretty damn good. You'll see the freshest seafood around, and plenty of interesting characters to boot.

# Roasted Crab Claws with Garlic Butter

**Serves:** 2
**Preparation time:** 10 minutes
**Cooking time:** 10 minutes

4 crab claws, approximately 4 inches long

sea salt and freshly ground black pepper

½ stick butter

3 garlic cloves, crushed

½ a lemon

1 sprig of fresh parsley, chopped

**To serve**

1 handful of watercress

1 teaspoon Sherry Dressing (see page 216)

fresh bread

If you've managed to get fresh crab claws, they will need to be boiled in salted water for 5 minutes, then refreshed in ice. If you couldn't make the voyage to Billingsgate and are using cooked or frozen claws, then skip this stage—just make sure you defrost them overnight.

Preheat your oven to 400°F. When ready to go, put an ovenproof skillet on the stove and heat it to a medium temperature.

Tap each claw firmly with the back of a knife, to create a crack. Do this between every joint. This is important, as it allows the butter to really get inside. Now put the claws, butter, and garlic into the hot pan and let things get started. Once the butter starts to foam, place the pan in the oven for 5 to 10 minutes, or until the claws are hot through.

Remove from the oven, squeeze the lemon juice over the claws, and season them with salt and pepper. Then lift the claws out and transfer to a serving plate. Give the garlicky butter a good stir, add the parsley, then pour it all over the crab. Garnish with the watercress, dressed with the sherry dressing, and serve with fresh bread.

Like the Smoked Haddock Scotch Eggs (opposite), this dish takes its inspiration from kedgeree. The chowder is more of a rainy-day variation, ideal for warming your cockles. We slow-cook our eggs at 145°F for 45 minutes, but if you don't have the equipment to regulate the temperature to precisely 145°F, you can cook a traditional poached egg.

# Smoked Haddock Chowder with a Poached Egg and Puffed Rice

**Serves:** 4
**Preparation time:** 20 minutes
**Cooking time:** 45 minutes

vegetable oil, for deep-frying

4 eggs

3 tablespoons olive oil

2 onions, minced

2 carrots, finely diced

2 stalks of celery, finely diced

1 leek, finely diced

4 potatoes, cut into ½-inch dice

1 bay leaf

sea salt and freshly ground black pepper

2 glasses of white wine

2 cups Chicken Stock (see page 216)

2 cups heavy cream

1 pound 5 ounces smoked haddock, skinned, boned, and cut into ½-inch cubes

1 handful of dry, parboiled long-grain rice (I use Uncle Ben's)

a pinch of curry powder

1 sprig of fresh parsley, chopped

1 leaf of fresh chives, chopped

1 sprig of fresh cilantro, chopped

Heat the vegetable oil to 350°F in your deep-fat fryer or in a deep heavy saucepan.

If slow-cooking the eggs, set your water bath to 145°F and, when the temperature is reached, add the eggs (in the shell) and let slow-cook for 45 minutes. You can use them immediately, or chill in iced water and refrigerate for later.

Heat the olive oil in a skillet and cook the onions, carrots, celery, leek, potatoes, and bay leaf until soft, with no color. Season with salt and pepper. Add the white wine and simmer until reduced by three-quarters, then add the chicken stock and continue to simmer until reduced by half.

Add the cream, bring to a simmer, then add the haddock and cook for approximately 15 minutes, or until the soup begins to thicken and the potatoes are cooked. Remove from the stove and set aside to cool if you're not eating right away.

To make the puffed rice, gently drop the parboiled rice into your deep-fat fryer or saucepan and after 30 seconds to 1 minute you will see it puff up like rice crispies. Remove the rice with a strainer and drain on paper towels. Sprinkle with salt and a pinch of curry powder.

Bring a saucepan of water to a boil for your eggs. Crack your slow-cooked eggs into the water and reheat, or poach your eggs in the traditional way.

To serve the chowder, remove the bay leaf, bring to a boil, add the chopped herbs, and divide between serving dishes. Place an egg in each one, then scatter with a good pinch of puffed rice. When eating, break the egg and give it a stir—it makes all the difference.

This is a dish that comes and goes at the restaurant, and our regulars love it when it makes a return. A play on kedgeree, one of the wonderful dishes the British brought back from India, it goes great with a hoppy IPA beer, of the same heritage, as extra hops were added to beer to make it last the voyage from England to Bombay.

# Smoked Haddock Scotch Egg with Curried Mayonnaise

**Makes:** 8

**Preparation time:** 2½ hours

**Cooking time:** 10 minutes

8 eggs

1 pound 5 ounces smoked haddock, skinned and boned

2 egg whites

pinch of sea salt

4 scallions, finely sliced

2 sprigs of fresh cilantro, chopped

2 small red chiles, seeded and chopped

½ teaspoon pickled ginger from a jar

a pinch of cayenne pepper

heaping ¾ cup all-purpose flour

2 eggs, beaten

2½ cups panko bread crumbs

vegetable oil, for deep-frying

**For the curried mayonnaise**

2 tablespoons Mayonnaise (see page 217)

a pinch of curry powder, lightly toasted

1 sprig of fresh cilantro, chopped

1 sprig of fresh mint, chopped

You will also need a deep-fat fryer

Cook the eggs in boiling water for 7 minutes, then refresh in iced water. Peel the eggs, then set aside.

Put the smoked haddock into a food processor with the egg whites and salt, and blend together. Transfer to a mixing bowl and add the scallions, cilantro, chiles, ginger, and cayenne pepper. You can reduce or omit the chiles and cayenne if you are not too enthusiastic on the spice front. Give it all a good stir.

Take a plum-size ball of the mixture, with wet hands to stop it from sticking, and flatten it out to approximately ½ inch thick. Wrap the haddock mixture around one of the peeled eggs, using a little more of the mixture if you need to fill any gaps. Repeat with the rest of the eggs. Place them on a plate lined with paper towels to absorb any moisture, and put into the fridge for 2 hours to firm up.

Get your flour, eggs, and bread crumbs ready in three separate bowls and remove the eggs from the fridge. Roll each one in the flour, then coat in the beaten eggs, and lastly roll in the bread crumbs.

Mix all the ingredients for the curried mayonnaise together in a bowl.

Heat the oil to 340°F in your deep-fat fryer and cook your Scotch eggs for 7 minutes, or until golden brown. Drain on paper towels then, when cool enough to handle, cut each one in half. Serve with a good dollop of curried mayonnaise.

Serves: 4

Preparation time: 30 minutes

Cooking time: 3 hours

### For the cuttlefish

2¼ pounds cuttlefish, cleaned

scant ½ cup olive oil, divided

2 onions, chopped

2 stalks of celery, chopped

1 carrot, chopped

1 head of fennel, chopped

2 bay leaves

1 sprig of fresh thyme

3 garlic cloves, crushed

1¼ cups red wine

1 (14-ounce) can of chopped tomatoes

Chicken Stock (see page 216), or enough to cover

### For the charred fennel

2 heads of fennel

3 tablespoons olive oil

2 garlic cloves, crushed

1 chile, seeded and roughly chopped

1 sprig of fresh rosemary

sea salt and freshly ground black pepper

### For the risotto

scant ½ cup olive oil

1 onion, minced

2 stalks of celery, finely diced

1 garlic clove, minced

1 red chile, seeded and finely chopped

1 sprig of fresh thyme

1 bay leaf

1¾ cups Arborio risotto rice

generous 2½ cups Chicken Stock (see page 216)

2 sprigs of fresh parsley, finely chopped

2 tablespoons chili oil

I love this dish—I learned how to cook cuttlefish when I did a two-week stage at the Anchor & Hope (one of the best gastro-pubs in the UK) located on The Cut near Waterloo station, in London. I don't remember their recipe exactly; I just remember the love and care that went into it. After making it at home for a few years, this is the recipe that works best (just don't forget the love). When in season, ramps instead of parsley at the end works wonderfully.

# Cuttlefish Risotto with Charred Fennel

Ask your fish dealer to prepare the cuttlefish for you, keeping the ink sac separate. Cut the cuttlefish into 2-inch pieces.

To cook the cuttlefish, heat 3 tablespoons of the olive oil in a skillet, add the onions, celery, carrot, fennel, bay leaves, thyme, and garlic, and cook gently until softened. Meanwhile, in another skillet, seal the cuttlefish in 3 tablespoons olive oil until lightly golden. When the vegetables are tender, add the red wine and simmer until reduced by half. Add the cuttlefish and the canned tomatoes and pour in enough chicken stock to cover. Bring to a boil, then lower the heat and let simmer.

At this point, carefully open the reserved ink sac (wearing gloves) and add to the stew. The ink will give it a beautiful deep color. Cover and cook for 1 hour, or until the cuttlefish is tender, then let cool in the stock. When cool, strain the cuttlefish, discarding the vegetables, and reserving the liquid for later.

To make the charred fennel, preheat your oven to 350°F and heat a ridged grill pan on the stove. Cut each piece of fennel into 8 segments and put them into a bowl with the olive oil, garlic, chile, and rosemary. Season and stir well. Griddle the fennel until dark, then transfer to a roasting pan with the garlic, oil, and chile from the bowl. Roast for 10 minutes, then remove from the oven and reserve for later.

To make the risotto, heat the olive oil and sweat the onion, celery, garlic, chile, thyme, and bay leaf, ensuring they don't color. Season with salt and pepper. Add the risotto rice and stir gently to coat in the olive oil. Now start adding the stock gradually, beginning with the cuttlefish stock and then, when that's finished, using the chicken stock, allowing the rice to absorb it all before you add more. You may not need to use all the chicken stock, depending on how much the cuttlefish stock has reduced when cooking.

As soon as the rice is tender, add the cuttlefish and bring up to temperature. Remove the bay leaf and thyme. Finish with the chopped parsley, then divide between serving plates and garnish each one with a piece of charred fennel and a drizzle of chili oil.

I was inspired to create this dish after tasting the smoked vodka from James Chase. He dropped off a sample bottle at the restaurant and it was such an interesting flavor that we started playing around with it, and naturally Russian flavors came to mind. Nonsmoked vodka works here as well, and you can try substituting the pickled cucumber with pickled beets, too.

# Mackerel Tartare with Smoked Vodka and Pickled Cucumber

**Serves:** 4

**Preparation time:** 20 minutes (if the cucumber is already pickled, otherwise 2 hours to 3 days)

**Cooking time:** none

¼ of a cucumber, peeled and seeded, cut into very fine dice

scant ½ cup Pickling Liquid (see page 216)

4 fresh mackerel fillets, skinned and boned

1 shallot, minced

1 leaf of fresh chives, finely chopped

1 tablespoon smoked vodka

sea salt

4 teaspoons crème fraîche

8 fresh cilantro leaves

sourdough bread, toasted

First, pickle your cucumber. This is best done 3 days in advance, but if you are short of time, a couple of hours will also be fine. Simply cover the cucumber with the pickling liquid and allow it to work its magic.

When ready to serve, slice the mackerel into ¼-inch cubes and place it in a mixing bowl. Drain the pickled cucumber and add to the bowl, then add the shallot, chives, and smoked vodka and season with salt.

Divide between serving plates, and finish each one with a teaspoon of crème fraîche and a cilantro leaf. Serve with fresh sourdough toast.

This is a dish from our opening restaurant menu and made me fall in love with n'duja—a spreadable spicy Calabrian sausage. It comes from Calabria in the south of Italy, and is almost as fiery as the people of the region—you can sneak it into pretty much any dish, and this one is no exception.

# Mussels and Clams with N'duja and Fennel Broth

**Serves:** 4
**Preparation time**: 20 minutes
**Cooking time**: 40 minutes

10½ ounces mussels
10½ ounces clams
5½ ounces n'duja, casing removed
olive oil
2 garlic cloves, crushed
3 shallots, minced
1 glass of white wine
4 sprigs of fresh parsley, chopped

**For the fennel broth**
8 heads of baby fennel, or 2 heads of regular fennel, sliced paper-thin
olive oil
2 cups Chicken Stock
(see page 216)
1 tablespoon Confit Shallots
(see page 217)
1 sprig of fresh thyme
1 bay leaf
10 fennel seeds, crushed
a pinch of saffron

Ask your fish dealer to clean your mussels and clams, removing the beards and any barnacles. Roll the n'duja into ½-inch balls.

Remove the herb tops from the fennel, chop them finely, and reserve for later.

To make the fennel broth, heat a drizzle of olive oil in a skillet, add the fennel, and cook until brown. Transfer to a saucepan, cover with the chicken stock, then add the other broth ingredients and simmer for 30 minutes.

When ready to serve, put a large saucepan over medium heat. Add a splash of olive oil, the mussels and clams, n'duja, garlic, and shallots and turn the heat up to high. As the n'duja starts to color, add the wine and let it reduce. Add the broth, including the fennel, and cook for a few minutes, or until all the mussels and clams have opened. Discard any that remain closed. Finish with chopped parsley and the chopped fennel tops.

Serves: 6
Preparation time: 1 day
Cooking time: 1 ½ hours

**For the salt cod**

¼ cup sea salt

finely grated zest of ½ a lemon

1 garlic clove, sliced

10½-ounce fresh cod fillet

1 sprig of fresh thyme

**For the brandade**

10½-ounce salt cod (see above)

2 cups milk

10½ ounces potatoes, peeled and cut into ¾-inch cubes

1 bay leaf

4 cloves of Confit Garlic (see page 217)

scant 1 cup olive oil

1 tablespoon capers, minced

1 sprig of fresh parsley, chopped

1 leaf of fresh chives, chopped

½ a lemon

**For the charred tomato jam**

6 plum tomatoes, halved

3 tablespoons olive oil, divided

2 shallots, minced

1 sprig of fresh thyme

1 sprig of fresh rosemary

2 garlic cloves, minced

1 chilli, halved, seeded, and minced

1 tablespoon tomato paste

¼ cup superfine sugar

3 tablespoons red wine vinegar

toasted bread, to serve

Based on the traditional French brandade de morue, this has been adapted a little: we use fresh cod that has been home-salted rather than the traditional salt cod, which is super dry and needs rehydrating for a few days, with regular water changes. This recipe is less aggressive than the French version, and we add capers and fresh herbs to jazz up the flavor a little. Buy the best olive oil you can—it makes all the difference.

# Whipped Brandade with Charred Tomato Jam

First, salt the fish, which needs to be started a day in advance. Sprinkle half the salt over the bottom of a bowl and add half the lemon zest and garlic. Set the fish on top, cover with the rest of the salt, lemon zest, and garlic, and add the thyme. Cover the bowl with plastic wrap and put into the fridge for 24 hours.

When you are ready to cook, preheat your oven to 400°F. Put the tomatoes into a roasting pan and drizzle with 1½ tablespoons of the olive oil. Place in the oven for about 20 minutes, or until the tomatoes start to blacken.

Heat the remaining 1½ tablespoons of olive oil in a saucepan, add the shallots, thyme, rosemary, garlic, and chile, and cook gently until soft, with no color. Add the tomatoes and tomato paste and cook for a further 10 minutes. Add the sugar and vinegar, then reduce the heat and let the mixture bubble away slowly until it is thick, like a jam (approximately 45 minutes). Remove from the heat, pass through a fine sieve, and let cool.

To make the brandade, take the cod from the fridge and wash off the salt under cold water. Dry with paper towels and place in a clean saucepan. Cover with the milk, then add the potatoes and the bay leaf. Let it simmer gently until the potatoes are cooked.

Strain the fish and potatoes and place in a mixing bowl. Add the garlic, then break it all down with a spoon until coarsely mashed. Slowly start adding the oil, beating it in. When all the oil has been absorbed, add the capers and herbs and a squeeze of lemon juice. Serve with freshly toasted bread, with the tomato jam on the side.

This dish is all about accentuating the pure flavors of the ingredients, by cooking them in a scallop shell sealed with bread dough, so none of them can escape. Try using pumpkin purée instead of mashed potatoes or, if you have bigger shells, add some clams. There are plenty of ways to vary this dish.

# Scallops Baked in the Shell

**Serves:** 4
**Preparation time:** 30 minutes
**Cooking time:** 1½ hours

1 onion, coarsely chopped

1 carrot, coarsely chopped

2 stalks of celery

¼ ounce dried Irish sea dulse

½ teaspoon saffron strands

1 bay leaf

2 cups Chicken Stock
(see page 216)

10 mussels, cleaned

2 potatoes, peeled and
cut into ¾-inch cubes

sea salt and freshly ground
black pepper

1½ tablespoons butter

4 hand-dived scallops,
in their shells

heaping ¾ cup all-purpose
flour mixed with just enough
water to bind

**To garnish**

fresh basil leaves

extra virgin olive oil

First, make the stock. Put the onion, carrot, celery, sea dulse, saffron, and bay leaf into a large saucepan, and add the chicken stock. Bring to a boil, then lower the heat and let simmer for 1 hour.

Strain the stock into a clean saucepan and bring back to a boil, then add the cleaned mussels and cook until they are all open (discard any that remain closed). Take out the mussels, pick the meat out of the shells, and set aside. Let the stock cool.

Next, make the mashed potatoes. Put the potatoes into a saucepan and cover with cold water. Add a good pinch of salt and gently bring to a simmer. When the potatoes are cooked, strain and purée. Add the butter and adjust the seasoning.

Use a shucking knife to prise the scallop shells apart and release the meat from the shells. Wash the scallops, then separate and discard the outer skirt, but keep the orange coral. Pat the white meat and coral dry on paper towels. Give your scallop shells a good scrub. Allow them to dry and put them on a baking pan.

Put a spoonful of the potato purée in the bottom of each shell, then place a raw scallop and coral on top, and a cooked mussel either side of the scallop. Pour 2 tablespoons of the stock over the scallop, and then place the other half of the scallop shell on top.

Take a piece of dough, the size of a plum, and roll it out in your hands until it's long enough to go around the circumference of the shell. Slowly work your way around the shell, making sure the lid is stuck to the base with the dough.

When ready to cook, preheat your oven to 350°F and cook the scallops for approximately 7 to 10 minutes. Cut through the baked dough to open the shell (be careful, they will be hot!). Ovens vary, so if the scallops come out a little undercooked, put them back in for a few extra minutes. Garnish with the basil leaves and drizzle with olive oil.

I love how the Spanish and Italians cook shellfish with cured meat—whether it be pancetta or pata negra—the two go so well together. You also find this in British cuisine, with bacon a wonderful substitute. Here we use two types of cured meat: guanciale, which is cured pig's cheek, and lardo, cured pig's fat from the back of the animal. The lardo melts into the bread crumbs to give a lovely piggy flavor, and, with the crunchiness, a nice texture as well. An Italian friend of mine once told me a wonderful thing about guanciale: "When God shaves, guanciale comes off and falls down to earth." Says it all really.

# Steamed Clams with Guanciale and a Lardo and Parsley Crumb

**Serves:** 4

**Preparation time:** 20 minutes

**Cooking time:** 20 minutes

2¾ ounces thinly sliced lardo, or Parma ham if you can't get hold of lardo

1²/₃ cups bread crumbs

2 pinches of chopped fresh parsley

8 slices of guanciale, or pancetta or Parma ham if you can't get hold of guanciale

1 tablespoon Confit Shallots (see page 217)

1 clove of Confit Garlic (see page 217)

1 sprig of fresh thyme

1 pound 5 ounces clams, cleaned

1 glass of white wine

scant ½ cup Chicken Stock (see page 216)

First make the lardo and parsley crumb. Heat a skillet over medium heat and add the lardo. Allow to cook so the fat is released, and when there is plenty of oil in the pan, add the bread crumbs and lower the heat. Cook slowly for about 10 minutes, or until all the fat is absorbed and the crumbs are evenly golden brown. Let cool, then add the parsley. Remove any unmelted pieces of lardo and discard.

When ready to serve, heat a saucepan over high heat. Add the guanciale and cook until golden brown. Next, add the shallots, garlic, and thyme. Give it a good stir, still over high heat, then add the clams and the white wine.

Let the wine reduce, then add the chicken stock and keep cooking until all the shells are open. (Discard any that remain closed.)

Serve in a big bowl, and sprinkled liberally with the lardo and parsley crumb.

This dish goes way back, to when Tom Cenci (our Senior Sous Chef) and I worked at Noble Rot, the sister restaurant to 1 Lombard Street, where we both trained. Julian, the chef, was one of the most influential people I have worked for—he's a loss to Britain, but a great gain for Canada, where he now cooks. We serve this a little differently at the restaurant to the way we did back then, but it's always a winner.

# Beef Carpaccio with Foie Gras

**Serves:** 6
**Preparation time:** 1 day
**Cooking time:** 30 minutes

1¼ cups port
¼ cup superfine sugar
1 clove
1 star anise
10½ ounces foie gras
sea salt and freshly ground black pepper
a splash of Cognac
center cut beef fillet weighing 1 pound 5 ounces, trimmed
1¾ ounces pecorino cheese

To make the port reduction, put the port, sugar, and spices into a small saucepan and heat until the mixture has the consistency of liquid honey. Strain and set aside to cool.

Next, we need to make the cured foie gras. Allow the foie gras to come to room temperature. Using a small spoon, start to explore inside and whenever you come across a vein, remove it. Shape it back together, place it on a plate, and season with salt, pepper, and a splash of Cognac. Put into the fridge for a couple of hours to firm up.

Preheat your oven to 250°F.

Put the foie gras into a baking dish and place in the oven for about 10 minutes, or until it just starts to melt. Remove it from the oven and lift it out of the melted fat, then place it on a piece of plastic wrap and roll it into a sausage about 1 inch thick, and the same length as your beef fillet. Tie each end and place in the freezer for a few hours until frozen. If you have more than one roll that's fine, you can freeze them for another time, or refrigerate and eat on toast.

Take your beef fillet and, using a wooden spoon or something similar, insert it down the center to make a hole all the way in so it comes out the other side. Give it a little wiggle to make the hole wider, as this is where we will insert the roll of foie gras. Remove the plastic wrap from the foie gras, then insert the roll into the hole in the beef. Seal the whole thing in plastic wrap again.

If you don't have a slicing machine, refrigerate the beef until firm, then carefully slice as thinly as possible. If you do have access to a slicing machine, freeze the beef overnight. When ready to serve, remove the beef from the freezer and allow to stand for 20 minutes (this will make it easier to slice). Slice the beef thinly.

Arrange the beef on a serving platter, about 8 slices per person, with the slices of foie gras on top. Drizzle with the port reduction and grate the pecorino finely and evenly all over it. Season with salt and pepper and enjoy.

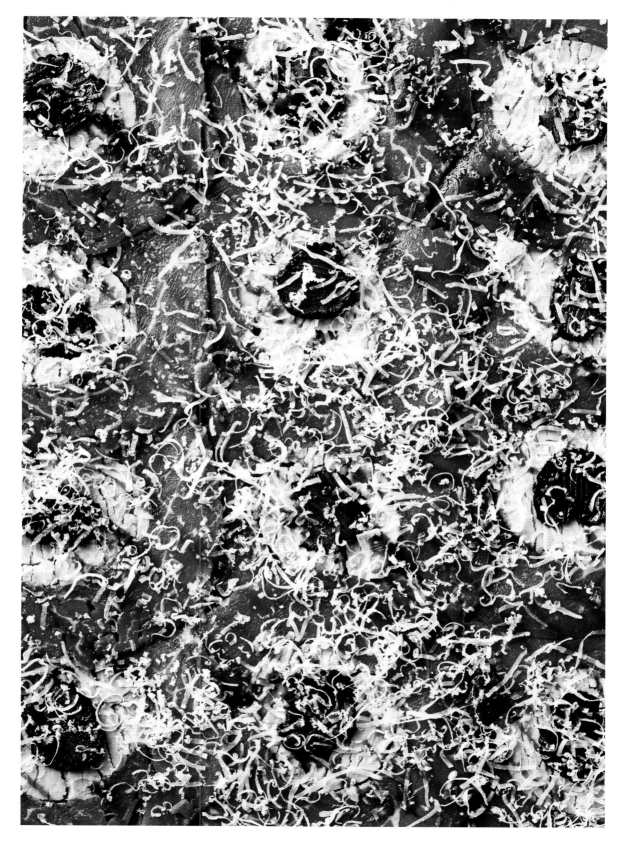

**Makes:** 15

**Preparation time:** 3 hours, plus cooling and chilling

**Cooking time:** 3½ hours

### For the apricot jam

1½ cups apricot purée

¼ cup superfine sugar

2 cardamom pods, bruised

### For the doughnut dough

½ cup superfine sugar

1 tablespoon dry active yeast

⅓ cup water

1⅔ pounds (6 cups) all-purpose flour

1 stick butter, softened

1½ cups + 2 tablespoons milk

vegetable oil, for deep-frying

### For the braised ox cheek

olive oil

2 ox cheeks, trimmed

1 onion, 1 carrot, and 1 celery stalk, each cut into ¾-inch pieces

2 garlic cloves, crushed

1 glass of red wine

1¾ cups Chicken Stock (see page 216)

1 bay leaf

1 sprig of fresh rosemary

1 sprig of fresh thyme

### For the ox cheek filling

1 pound 2 ounces braised ox cheek, shredded

3½ ounces aji panca paste

¼ of a bunch each of fresh cilantro and fresh mint, chopped

⅔ cup cream cheese

scant 1 cup Sriracha hot sauce

sea salt and freshly ground black pepper

### For the smoked paprika sugar

¼ cup superfine sugar

1 teaspoon smoked paprika

You will also need a deep-fat fryer

This is one of the dishes that got people talking, but not everyone loves it. It was awarded the number 1 reason to eat out by *Waitrose Kitchen* magazine, which was a great achievement for our humble little doughnut, and one we are all very proud of. We make a spicy filling with slow-braised ox cheek, mix it with cream cheese and various herbs and spices; then, in true doughnut style, we roll them in sugar. But not just any sugar—smoked paprika sugar.

# Spicy Ox Cheek Doughnuts with Apricot Jam

To make the apricot jam, put everything in a small saucepan over medium heat and cook for 20 minutes, or until it has a jamlike consistency. Discard the cardamom pods and let the jam cool before serving. Keep in the fridge for up to 1 week.

To make the dough, mix the sugar and yeast in a bowl with the water and set aside for 10 minutes. Rub the flour and butter together, then add the yeast mixture and the milk and knead for 5 minutes. Put the dough into a clean bowl, cover, and refrigerate for 30 minutes to 1 hour to firm up.

Preheat your oven to 320°F.

Heat a drizzle of olive oil in a skillet and seal the ox cheeks until brown. Transfer them to a Dutch oven. Add the onion, carrot, celery, and garlic to the skillet and cook gently until tender, with a little color. Add the wine and simmer until reduced by three-quarters, then pour the contents of the skillet over the ox cheeks. Add the chicken stock and herbs. Put the lid on the Dutch oven and place in the oven for approximately 3 hours, or until the cheeks give way when pressed with a spoon. Let stand in the stock and, when cool enough to handle, take out and break down the meat by shredding with your fingers.

To prepare the ox cheek filling, mix all the ingredients together. Roll into golfball-size balls and refrigerate for 30 minutes to firm up again.

Remove the dough from the fridge. To make the doughnuts, divide the dough into 15 equal-size pieces. Take one piece, flatten it out, then put a ball of the ox cheek mixture in the middle and wrap the dough around it. Make all the doughnuts this way, then put them into the fridge to rest for 30 minutes.

When ready to cook, heat the vegetable oil to 340°F in your deep-fat fryer. Take the doughnuts out of the fridge and make sure they are completely sealed all the way around. Let stand for 10 minutes to prove a little, then cook in batches for 10 minutes, turning them over after 5 minutes, until dark golden.

Mix the sugar and paprika together and, when the doughnuts are cooked, roll them in the sugar mixture just before serving. Serve with the apricot jam.

I love using mutton, and so should a lot more people. It's great for the farming industry, which needs all the help it can get. Mutton has a reputation for being tough, but that's really not the case—it's just like lamb but with a more intense, grown-up flavor. These sliders are incredibly popular at the restaurant, and you can make them as big or as small as you like. Feel free to add some Little Gem leaves if you like, along with some whole mint and cilantro leaves, and a few ultra-thin slices of red onion, especially if making them normal burger size.

# Harissa-spiced Mutton Slider with Lime Crème Fraîche

**Makes:** 12

**Preparation time:** 30 minutes, plus cooling

**Cooking time:** 1½ hours

12 slider-sized burger buns, approximately 2 inches wide

Charred Tomato Jam (see page 94)

### For the sliders

1 teaspoon olive oil or vegetable oil

1 onion, minced

1 garlic clove, minced

3½ tablespoons harissa paste

1 red chile, seeded and minced

1 teaspoon smoked paprika

1 pound 2 ounces ground mutton (or lamb)

1 sprig of fresh cilantro, chopped

1 sprig of fresh mint, chopped

### For the lime crème fraîche

¼ cup crème fraîche

juice of ½ a lime

finely grated zest of 1 lime

To make the sliders, heat the oil in a skillet and sweat the onion and garlic gently for 8 to 10 minutes, or until soft but with no color. Add the harissa, chile, and paprika and cook for a further 5 minutes. Let cool, then put into a bowl, add the ground mutton and herbs, and mix well. Shape the mixture into 12 small patties approximately 2 inches wide and ¾ inch thick and refrigerate until ready to cook.

To make the lime crème fraîche, mix the ingredients together and refrigerate.

When ready to serve, heat a ridged grill pan or a skillet over high heat and cook the patties for 2 to 3 minutes on each side.

Split and lightly toast the buns, then add a teaspoon of crème fraîche on one side and a teaspoon of tomato jam on the other. Add the patties and serve.

This is perfect for an afternoon snack, or as something you can eat when you get home after a night out. The chutney recipe came from my time at the Old Brewery in Greenwich, where we used beer in a lot of our dishes, whether it be cooking with the different styles or using the actual ingredients—hops, barley, even recycling the yeast that is skimmed from the top of the tanks.

# Rabbit Rillettes with Beer Chutney

**Serves:** 6

**Preparation time:** 1 day

**Cooking time:** 3 hours

### For the rillettes

1 pound rabbit legs (approximately 2 legs)

2 tablespoons sea salt

1 sprig of fresh rosemary

1 sprig of fresh thyme

2½ cups duck fat (or enough to cover), melted

1 cup cream cheese

1 stick butter, softened

¼ cup Dijon mustard

### For the beer chutney

generous ¾ pound apples (approximately 3 to 4 apples), peeled, cored, and cut into ½-inch pieces

scant 1 cup raisins

1 onion, minced

1 tablespoon mustard seeds

1 tablespoon ground ginger

½ cup white wine vinegar

½ cup porter (dark brown, strongly flavored beer)

1¼ cups light brown sugar

### To serve

sourdough bread, toasted

¼ cup pistachios, roasted and crushed

To make the rillettes, put the rabbit legs into a dish. Mix the salt and herbs together and sprinkle all over the rabbit. Cover and leave in the fridge overnight.

When ready to cook, preheat your oven to 265°F.

Brush the salt off of the rabbit, and place the legs in a Dutch oven. Add the duck fat and place in the oven for approximately 3 hours, or until the meat falls off of the bone. Remove from the oven and let cool in the fat.

Remove the legs from the fat, and pick the meat from the bones. Put it into a fresh bowl, add the cream cheese, butter, and mustard, and beat together, mixing really well.

To make the chutney, put the apples, raisins, onion, mustard seeds, and ginger into a large saucepan and cook gently until soft. Add the vinegar, beer, and sugar, reduce the heat to low, and cook for approximately 2 to 3 hours, or until all is reduced and shiny.

Serve the rillettes spread on toast, with the chutney on top and scattered with some crushed pistachios.

After testing various marinades for lamb and mutton, Adi, one of our managers, described what we came up with as "Hara bhara," which translates as "fresh and green" in Hindi. I love that description, so we called it that on the menu. It's a very herby marinade with a subtle spice that works really well with the smoky eggplant and is nicely cut by the yogurt.

# Hara Bhara Lamb with Smoky Eggplant and Mint Yogurt

**Serves:** 4
**Preparation time:** 1 day
**Cooking time:** 1 ½ hours

8 lamb cutlets

3 eggplants

4 cloves of Confit Garlic (see page 217)

1 teaspoon cumin seeds, toasted

1 sprig of fresh thyme

sea salt and freshly ground black pepper

⅓ cup organic plain yogurt

10 fresh mint leaves, finely chopped

**For the marinade**

¼ of a bunch of fresh cilantro

¼ of a bunch of fresh mint

a large pinch of fresh parsley

2 jalapeño chiles

a ¼-inch piece of fresh ginger

grated zest of ¼ of a lemon

½ teaspoon ground coriander

½ teaspoon ground cumin

seeds from 2 cardamom pods

approximately 3 tablespoons olive oil

For the lamb marinade, place all the ingredients except the olive oil in a food processor and pulse, adding the oil in small quantities at a time, until a pesto-like paste is formed. Massage the paste into the lamb cutlets and let marinate overnight in the refrigerator.

When ready to cook, preheat your oven to 350°F.

Heat a ridged grill pan and when hot, add the whole eggplants and char all over until almost burned.

Place them in a roasting pan and put into the oven for about 30 minutes, or until soft. Let cool, then carefully peel off the skin, keeping only the flesh. Place the flesh in a food processor and add the garlic, cumin, thyme (leaves only), salt, and pepper. Blitz until smooth, then transfer the mixture to a saucepan and cook over very low heat for a further 30 minutes, or until dried out a little.

In the meantime, mix together the yogurt and mint, season with salt and pepper, and set aside.

Take the cutlets out of the marinade and season them. Cook them in a ridged grill pan over medium heat for approximately 3 minutes on each side. Serve with the smoky eggplant purée and a dollop of mint yogurt.

After having a beautiful pine tree on display for Christmas, it seemed a waste to throw it away come January, so I picked all the needles off and dried them out for a few days. We then created a wild venison dish and served it alongside a small pile of the pine needles—these had been set on fire and reduced to embers, which had an amazing aroma. Not only is it a nice bit of theater, but it makes sense as well: Scottish deer in the forest among the pine trees, Christmas, bonfires... If you don't have a real pine tree, try using rosemary, which works great, too.

# Venison Carpaccio with Pear, Almonds, and Pine Embers

**Serves:** 6

**Preparation time:** 30 minutes (3 hours if drying the rosemary)

**Cooking time:** none

14-ounce venison fillet steak, trimmed

1 ripe pear, peeled and cut into ½-inch dice

1 tablespoon Confit Shallots (see page 217)

20 whole almonds, roasted and crushed

scant ½ cup olive oil

2 tablespoons sherry vinegar

1 sprig of fresh cilantro, chopped

sea salt and freshly ground black pepper

dried pine needles, or rosemary dried in an oven on low heat or a just-used oven for a few hours

Slice the venison as thinly as possible. Arrange the slices over one side of a serving dish, leaving the other side empty for the pine needles.

Put the pear, confit shallots, almonds, olive oil, sherry vinegar, and cilantro into a bowl and stir to combine. Season with salt and pepper, then spoon the mixture over the sliced venison.

On the other side of the serving dish add a little pile of pine needles. When ready to serve, use a lighter to set the pine needles on fire. The flame will disappear after a few seconds and a wonderful aroma will be produced.

This is what I call beer food, perfect with a chilled lager on a Sunday afternoon; the chicken necks can be prepped well in advance. Best to ask your butcher for these, as most supermarkets won't have them. An amazing snack that costs very little.

# Crispy Chicken Necks with Chile and Garlic

**Makes:** enough for 4 snacks
**Preparation time:** 1 day
**Cooking time:** 1 ¼ hours

1 pound 2 ounces chicken necks

¼ of a bunch of fresh parsley

¼ of a bunch of fresh thyme

¼ of a bunch of fresh rosemary

½ cup + 1 ½ tablespoons superfine sugar

scant ½ cup salt

duck fat, to cover

vegetable oil, for deep-frying

all-purpose flour, for dusting

## To serve

¼ teaspoon dried red pepper flakes

2 cloves of Confit Garlic (see page 217)

sea salt and freshly ground black pepper

a pinch of chopped fresh parsley

a pinch of chopped fresh chives

a squeeze of lemon juice

You will also need a deep-fat fryer

The day before you want to make these, put the chicken necks into a bowl. Finely chop the parsley, thyme, and rosemary and mix with the sugar and salt. Sprinkle all over the chicken necks, then cover and refrigerate overnight.

When ready to cook, preheat your oven to 265°F.

Remove the chicken necks from the marinade and place them in a baking dish. Cover them with duck fat and place in the oven for about 1½ hours, or until the meat on the necks pulls away from the bone. Let cool in the fat, then take the necks out of the fat and refrigerate if not eating right away.

When ready to cook, heat the oil to 350°F in your deep-fat fryer. Lightly dust the necks with flour, then fry in batches for about 3 minutes, or until crisp. Drain on paper towels.

Put the red pepper flakes, confit garlic, seasoning, and herbs into a bowl and mix gently with a spoon so that the garlic cloves break up a little.

Remove the necks from the deep-fat fryer, add to the seasoning bowl, and stir well. Finish with a squeeze of lemon juice and serve immediately.

**Serves:** 6

**Preparation time:** 1 day

**Cooking time:** 4½ hours

4 Barbecued Spiced Pig's Ears
(see page 194)

heaping ¾ cup all-purpose flour,
divided

2 eggs, divided, beaten

1²/₃ cups bread crumbs, divided

vegetable oil, for deep-frying

sea salt and freshly ground
black pepper

½ a lemon

1 recipe Spice Mix (see page 194)

**For the hog jowl nuggets**

8 hog jowls, trimmed

olive oil

½ an onion, ½ a carrot, and 1 stalk
of celery, all cut into ¾-inch pieces

2 garlic cloves, crushed

1 sprig of fresh thyme

1 sprig of fresh rosemary

1 bay leaf

1 glass of red wine

3¼ cups Chicken Stock
see page 216)

½ cup grated Parmesan cheese

1 sprig of fresh parsley, chopped

1 tablespoon Confit Shallots
(see page 217)

**For the pig's tails**

6 pig's tails

½ an onion, cut into ¾-inch pieces

½ a carrot, cut into ¾-inch pieces

1 stalk of celery, cut into ¾-inch
pieces

2 garlic cloves, crushed

1 sprig of fresh thyme

1 sprig of fresh rosemary

1 bay leaf

1 glass of red wine

3¼ cups Chicken Stock
(see page 216)

You will also need a deep-fat fryer

Inspired by the traditional fritto misto of Italy, this is my take on it, but porkified. A great dish for a night in front of the TV, or an appetizer for the table to tuck right into, it's cheap and fun to see how tasty these forgotten cuts can be. You can even throw in a few "quavers" from page 199.

# Piggy Fritto Misto

Follow the Day 1 method for the pig's ears on page 194.

For the hog jowl nuggets, heat a drizzle of olive oil in a skillet and sear the hog jowls until golden brown. Place the jowls in a saucepan. Add the onion, carrot, celery, and garlic to the skillet and cook gently for about 5 minutes. Add to the hog jowls, along with the thyme, rosemary, and bay leaf. Deglaze the pan with the red wine, and simmer until reduced by half. Pour over the jowls, and cover with the chicken stock. Cook over low heat for approximately 4 hours, or until the jowls are tender and break down very easily when squeezed. Let cool in the stock.

Meanwhile, cook the pig's tails: Preheat the oven to 250°F. Place all the pig's tails ingredients in a baking dish, cover with foil and place in the oven for approximately 3 hours, or until the meat gives when squeezed. Let cool in the stock, as with the cheeks, and when cool remove, drain, and refrigerate. When chilled, dust with half the flour, roll in one of the beaten eggs, and coat with half of bread crumbs, then set aside for later.

When cool, remove the hog jowls from the stock and flake into a mixing bowl. Strain the stock into another saucepan and simmer until reduced to a glaze with a consistency like honey. Add to the flaked jowls and mix well. Add the Parmesan, parsley, and confit shallots and mix well. Roll into grape-size balls and place in the fridge to firm up. When firm, dust with the remaining flour, roll in the remaining beaten egg, and coat with rest of the bread crumbs, then set aside for later.

When ready to eat, heat the oil to 350°F in your deep-fat fryer and dust the pig's ears with flour. Fry the tails first for about 6 minutes, or until golden brown and hot inside, then drain on paper towels. Next fry the ears and nuggets for 3 to 4 minutes. Drain well and place everything on a serving plate.

Season the tails and nuggets with salt and a squeeze of lemon juice, and for the ears use the spice mix on page 194 to season separately.

**Makes:** 8

**Preparation time:** 2 hours

**Cooking time:** 45 minutes

1 pound 2 ounces puff pastry

all-purpose flour, for dusting

eggwash (2 eggs beaten with 3 tablespoons milk)

**For the sausage mix**

7 ounces Middle White pork (or any other heirloom-breed pork you can get), ground

3½ ounces foie gras, veins removed, cut into ½-inch cubes

2 Cumberland or other high-quality pork sausages, casing removed

scant 1 cup bread crumbs

1 sprig of fresh parsley, chopped

¼ cup Confit Shallots (see page 217)

4 cloves of Confit Garlic (see page 217)

1 sprig of fresh thyme, leaves only

8 Agen prunes, soaked in brandy overnight and chopped into ½-inch pieces

sea salt and freshly ground black pepper

**For the lentils**

olive oil

1 onion, minced

1 stalk of celery, finely diced

1 carrot, finely diced

1 sprig of fresh thyme

1 cup Puy lentils

2 cups Chicken Stock (see page 216)

2 sprigs of fresh parsley, finely chopped

3 tablespoons sherry vinegar

1½ tablespoons butter

2½ tablespoons all-purpose flour

Being English, sausage rolls have always been a part of my life since I was a kid, and it was only a matter of time before I started playing around with them. This is a recipe I started cooking back in 2008 at the Ambassador, which went down really well with our guests.

# Middle White Pork Sausage Rolls with Prunes and Lentils

First, make the sausage mixture. Mix all ingredients together and season with salt and pepper.

On a floured surface, roll out the pastry as thin as a dime and cut it into 8 rectangles, each 6 x 4 inches. Take one rectangle at a time. On one half, spoon the mixture in a sausage-like line down the longer side. Brush eggwash all around, then fold the pastry over and seal with a fork. Set on a cookie sheet lined with nonstick parchment paper, and make 3 cuts in the top of the pastry for the steam to escape. Refrigerate for at least 30 minutes so the pastry can firm up.

Preheat your oven to 350°F.

For the lentils, heat a splash of olive oil in a saucepan over medium heat. Add the onion, celery, carrot, and thyme, and cook gently without coloring. Add the lentils and the stock and simmer for approximately 20 minutes, or until the lentils are cooked. Add the parsley and sherry vinegar and season with salt and pepper.

Mix the butter and flour together to form a paste, roll it into small balls, and drop them into the lentils. Turn the heat up and stir well. As the butter and flour melt, the mixture will begin to thicken. Cook for a further 5 minutes.

Take the sausage rolls out of the fridge and brush eggwash on the tops and sides. Place them in the middle of the oven and cook for about 20 to 25 minutes, or until golden brown. Serve in bowls, with the lentils on the bottom and the sausage rolls on top.

Back in the days when everyone had fires roaring in the winter, and the mist and fog of the Thames Valley combined with the smoke, the result was often referred to as a pea souper, which later became London Particular. Nowadays, the idiom is reversed and we call pea and ham soup "London Particular." Peas and ham, ham and eggs—both present themselves as obvious garnishes, so we use both for this winter warmer.

# London Particular

**Serves:** 8

**Preparation time:** 30 minutes, plus cooling

**Cooking time:** 4 hours

2½ cups dried split peas (follow package instructions for soaking)

1 smoked ham hock

1 onion, peeled and left whole

2 stalks of celery, chopped

1 bay leaf

1 sprig of fresh thyme

sea salt and freshly ground black pepper

vegetable oil, for frying

8 slow-cooked eggs (see page 86) or regular poached eggs

all-purpose flour, for dusting

2 handfuls of pea shoots

6 fresh mint leaves, finely sliced

Put the split peas, ham hock, onion, celery, bay leaf, and thyme into a large saucepan and add water to cover. Bring to a boil, then lower the heat and cook for approximately 3½ hours, skimming regularly, until the meat comes away from the bone of the ham hock. The peas may stick to the bottom, so stir frequently and top off with water as necessary. The final consistency should be that of a thick soup.

Remove the ham hock and let cool. In the meantime, remove the bay leaf and thyme and discard, then blend the soup in a food processor until smooth. Correct the seasoning. When the ham hock is cool, take the meat off of the bone and flake it into small strands. Pat dry with paper towels.

Heat the oil to 350°F in your deep-fat fryer or in a heavy saucepan.

Bring a saucepan of water to a boil. Either reheat your slow-cooked eggs or poach your eggs traditionally in the water. Meanwhile, gently reheat your soup.

Dust a handful of the ham flakes with flour and fry until crisp (this should only take 2 minutes), then drain and set aside for garnishing.

Put some of the flaked ham in the bottom of each serving bowl, about a tablespoon per person. Fill the bowl with soup, put an egg on top, and season with salt and pepper. Garnish with the pea shoots, finely sliced mint leaves, and the crispy ham.

**Serves:** 4

**Preparation time:** 1 hour, plus resting

**Cooking time:** 2 hours

**For the endive marmalade**

2 tablespoons vegetable oil

4 heads of red Belgian endive, sliced into matchstick-size pieces

1 onion, finely sliced

2 cloves of Confit Garlic (see page 217)

½ a glass of red wine

½ a glass of port

grated zest and juice of 3 oranges

1 sprig of fresh thyme

1 sprig of fresh rosemary

2 tablespoons superfine sugar

1 star anise

sea salt and freshly ground black pepper

juice of 3 oranges

generous ¼ cup walnut oil

2 onions, peeled and halved

3 garlic cloves, crushed but unpeeled

2 carrots, peeled and halved lengthwise

2 bay leaves

1 sprig of fresh thyme

2 sprigs of fresh sage

piece of pork belly, weighing 1 pound 2 ounces, scored

olive oil

1¾ cups Chicken Stock (see page 216)

12 walnut halves, roasted

watercress, to garnish

I absolutely adore pig in any form, but pork belly remains king; so juicy and tender. This is served with a bittersweet endive marmalade, which cuts the fat nicely. Very much a small plate—you can adjust the dish and add creamy mashed potatoes and maybe some sprouting broccoli, but keep the marmalade or it could become too rich.

# Crispy Pork Belly with Endive Marmalade, Orange, and Walnuts

To make the endive marmalade, heat the vegetable oil in a large saucepan. Add the endives, onion, and garlic and cook gently until soft and lightly colored.

Put the red wine, port, orange zest and juice, thyme, rosemary, sugar, and star anise into another saucepan and bring to a boil, then lower the heat and simmer for 15 minutes to infuse the flavors. Strain, then pour the liquid into the pan of endive and onion and turn the heat to medium. Season with salt and pepper and cook slowly for about 45 minutes, or until the mixture has reduced to the consistency of jam.

Put the orange juice into a small saucepan and bring to a boil, then lower the heat and let simmer until it has reduced by about three-quarters and is almost a caramel. Gradually whisk in the walnut oil until it emulsifies, then set aside for later.

To cook the pork belly, preheat your oven to 400°F.

Put the onions, garlic, carrots, and herbs into a roasting pan. Put the pork joint on top, drizzle with olive oil, and season well. Roast in the oven for about 30 minutes, or until the crackling begins to form, at which point reduce the temperature to 300°F. Add the stock and continue roasting for another hour or so, then remove from the oven and let the pork rest for 30 minutes.

Slice the skin off of the pork, and if it is not crisp, place it back in the oven for 10 minutes or so. If it is crisp, slice it into ½-inch strips. Strain the liquid from the roasting pan and reserve.

Carve a nice slice of pork for each person, add a spoonful of marmalade, scatter with a few crushed walnuts, and serve with a couple of slices of crackling. Finish with a spoonful of the roasting juices and some watercress, dressed with the orange and walnut emulsion.

This dish, while a tad tricky to prepare, has a great wow factor. We remove the bones from the fish, leaving the head and tail intact, with the belly left in, so the fish is used as a basket for the fresh summer vegetables to sit inside. At the restaurant, as the seasons change, we adapt the garnish, using ingredients such as wild mushrooms, Jerusalem artichokes, asparagus, and ramps.

# Whole Baked Sea Bass with Zucchini, Baby Potatoes, and Peas

**Serves:** 2

**Preparation time:** 45 minutes

**Cooking time:** 1 hour

1 sea bass (approximately 2¼ pounds), left whole, scaled (ask your fish dealer to "canoe cut" it, or see the method below)

olive oil

sea salt and freshly ground black pepper

1 stick butter

10 new potatoes, cooked and skins removed

⅔ cup shelled fresh peas, blanched and refreshed

2 zucchini, diced, blanched, and refreshed

scant 1 cup Chicken Stock (see page 216)

10 fresh mint leaves, finely sliced

2 plum tomatoes, peeled, seeded, and cut into ½-inch cubes

watercress or pea shoots, to garnish

½ a lemon

If preparing the fish yourself, fillet it from the back down, but don't cut through the stomach cavity. When completed on both sides, take a pair of scissors and snip the bone behind the head and at the tail, so you can remove all the bones. Take out all the guts, and remove the bloodline, fins, and gills. Give the fish a really good wash. Pat dry with paper towels, and remove any tiny bones.

Preheat your oven to 350°F. Place the fish, belly-side down and with the fillets opened out, on a baking pan lined with oiled nonstick parchment paper. Drizzle with olive oil, season with salt and pepper, and place in the oven—it should take about 10 to 15 minutes to cook.

In the meantime, heat the butter in a large skillet. When foaming, add the potatoes, peas, and zucchini and give them a good sauté. Season, then slowly add the chicken stock, 1 ladleful at a time, allowing it to reduce before adding more. At the end you should have a buttery, emulsified sauce around the vegetables. Finish with the mint and chopped tomatoes.

Remove the fish from the oven, and carefully lift it off of the pan with a spatula and transfer to a serving dish. Pour the vegetables into the cavity of the fish. Garnish with some watercress or pea shoots if you like, and squeeze the lemon over it.

Use whatever fish is fresh and at its best on the day—the ones I've listed below are great, but are only an example. Monkfish, pollock, mackerel, and sea bream are all good. If you can find them, garnish with any sea vegetables—samphire, sea rosemary, sea purslane—you can get your hands on.

# Seared Dayboat Fish Stew with Spring Vegetables

**Serves:** 4
**Preparation time:** 20 minutes
**Cooking time:** 1½ hours

olive oil

1 onion, cut into ½-inch dice

2 stalks of celery, cut into ½-inch dice

1 leek, cut into ½-inch dice

1 sprig of fresh thyme

2 bay leaves

¼ of a bunch of fresh parsley, stalks and leaves separated

2¼ pounds fish bones, cleaned and washed

2 glasses of white wine

3 pints water

10½ ounces mussels

10½ ounces clams

20 leaves of fresh chives, cut into 1-inch batons

1 stick butter

2 sea bass fillets, each one cut in half

4 pieces of cod, approximately 3½ ounces each, skin on

sea salt and freshly ground black pepper

1 bunch of baby carrots, trimmed, blanched, and refreshed

1 bunch of baby turnips, trimmed, blanched, and refreshed

1 bunch of baby leeks, trimmed, blanched, and refreshed

Heat a little olive oil in a large saucepan and add the onion, celery, leek, thyme, bay leaves, and parsley stalks. Cook gently for 10 to 12 minutes, or until softened but with no color, then add the fish bones and cook for a further 10 minutes.

Add the wine and cook until reduced by three-quarters. Add about 3 pints of cold water, or enough to cover, then bring to a boil. Lower the heat and let simmer for 30 minutes, skimming frequently. Strain away as many vegetables as possible and all of the fish bones, then pour the broth back into the saucepan and simmer until reduced by half.

When ready to eat, heat the broth and add the mussels, clams, parsley leaves, and chives. Add the butter and let it melt and enrich the broth.

Heat a little olive oil in a skillet. Season the sea bass and cod with salt and pepper, add to the pan and cook, skin-side down, or until the skin is crisp.

Add the blanched vegetables to the broth, and let reheat for 3 to 4 minutes. Discard any mussels and clams that remain closed. Pour the stew into a large serving bowl, and place the seared fish on top. Garnish with sea vegetables, if you have them.

Salt-baking is a great technique, with both theater and impressive results. While the salt bakes it comes together to form a thick crust, so that as the fish bakes the steam that's released, rather than escaping, is absorbed back into the fish, keeping it juicy. The aromats release all their beautiful flavors, so your kitchen will smell amazing. The ones we use here are just a guideline. You can use whatever tickles your fancy. Use whatever vegetables are in season, and if you can't find dried seaweed use a selection of fresh soft herbs instead.

# Salt-baked Sea Bream with Market Vegetables and Seaweed Butter Sauce

**Serves:** 2
**Preparation time:** 20 minutes
**Cooking time:** 40 minutes

seeds from 2 cardamom pods

a pinch of fennel seeds

a pinch of fenugreek seeds

a pinch of coriander seeds

10 juniper berries

2 star anise

2 cloves

scant 1 cup sea salt

2 egg whites, beaten until stiff

1 whole sea bream, scaled and gutted, fins and gills removed

olive oil

1 shallot, minced

finely grated zest and juice of 2 lemons

1 stick butter, cubed

sea salt and freshly ground black pepper

a pinch of dried Irish sea dulse, rehydrated and minced

2 heads of baby fennel, blanched and refreshed

1 bunch of baby leeks, blanched and refreshed

1 bunch of baby carrots, blanched and refreshed

Preheat your oven to 350°F.

To make the salt crust, mix all the spices together in a bowl, then add the salt and the beaten egg white, and fold in to form a paste. Place your sea bream on a lightly oiled baking pan lined with nonstick parchment paper and spread the salt crust over the skin, leaving the head and tail exposed. The crust should be about ¾ to 1¼ inches thick. Bake in the oven for approximately 25 to 30 minutes. To tell if it is ready, insert a flat-edged knife into the thickest part of the fish. After a few seconds remove the knife and the blade should feel hot to touch.

Meanwhile, heat a little olive oil in a skillet and cook the shallot gently until soft. Add the lemon juice and cook until reduced by half, then slowly add the butter, a few cubes at a time, whisking as you go so that the sauce emulsifies. Season with salt and pepper, then add the lemon zest and seaweed (or herbs, see introduction) and give it a good stir. Set aside and keep warm.

When ready to serve, reheat your vegetables and the sauce, and season with salt and pepper. Remove the fish from the oven, and let rest for 5 minutes. Slide the fish onto a serving dish and take to the table. Carefully lift off the salt crust and discard. Remove and discard the skin from the fish and serve with the vegetables, along with the sauce in a pitcher on the side.

Another example of mixing cured pork with shellfish, and one that can be easily modified to make a soup. If ramps aren't in season, try adding a clove or two of confit garlic at the end (see page 217), and add some parsley in place of the ramp leaves.

# Baked Cod with Clam Chowder and Bacon

**Serves:** 2

**Preparation time:** 20 minutes

**Cooking time:** 1 hour 15 minutes

8 strips of smoked bacon, very finely sliced into lardons

1 onion, finely diced

1 garlic clove, finely diced

1 sprig of fresh thyme

1 bay leaf

scant 1 cup heavy cream

scant 1 cup Chicken Stock (see page 216)

2 potatoes, peeled and cut into ½-inch dice

2 portions of cod, approximately 5¾ ounces each, skin on

olive oil

sea salt and freshly ground black pepper

4 wild ramp leaves, cut into ¾-inch pieces

**For the clams**

10½ ounces clams

1 glass of white wine

1 shallot, diced

1 garlic clove, crushed

1 sprig of fresh thyme

First, cook the clams. Put the clams, white wine, shallot, garlic, and thyme into a mixing bowl. Heat a medium saucepan, and when it's hot, add the contents of the bowl and cover immediately. After 2 to 3 minutes the clams will open, at which point take the pan off of the heat and strain, reserving the stock. Discard any clams that don't open. Pass the stock through a fine sieve, or, better still, a clean dish towel, to remove any grit, as the stock will be used for the chowder. Pick the meat out of most of the clam shells, saving a few in the shell for a garnish.

Preheat your oven to 350°F.

Heat a medium saucepan and add the bacon. Cook gently until golden brown, pouring away any fat that comes out. Keep scraping the bottom of the pan—that's where all the flavor is. Add the onion, garlic, thyme, and bay leaf and cook gently until soft.

Now add the clam stock and simmer until reduced by three-quarters. Add the cream, chicken stock, and diced potatoes and cook for about 20 minutes, or until the potatoes are cooked. Watch that it doesn't stick to the bottom of the pan.

Put the cod on a baking pan lined with nonstick parchment paper, drizzle with olive oil, and season with salt and pepper. Bake in the oven for about 8 to 10 minutes, or until just cooked through.

To serve, remove the thyme and bay leaf from the chowder, add the clams and the ramps or, if using, confit garlic and herbs (see introduction), and let cook for a few minutes. Taste and correct the seasoning at this stage.

Serve in large bowls with the cod, seasoned with salt and pepper on top, with the clams in the shell in full view.

Being such a robust fish, monkfish is a great match for earthy flavors such as wild mushrooms, Jerusalem artichokes, and salsify. This dish is perfect for the fall, and the addition of smoked butter really brings the ingredients together. If you can't get hold of trompette mushrooms, mixed wild mushrooms are fine. Pancetta would also work well here. Now there's food for thought.

# Roast Monkfish with Salsify and Jerusalem Artichokes

**Serves:** 2
**Preparation time:** 20 minutes
**Cooking time:** 45 minutes

vegetable oil, for deep-frying

1 handful of Jerusalem artichokes, peeled and cut into ¾-inch slices

2 sticks of salsify, peeled and sliced on an angle into ¾-inch pieces

sea salt and freshly ground black pepper

juice of ½ a lemon

olive oil

2 portions of monkfish, approximately 7 ounces each, on the bone, membrane removed

1 stick butter, plus a little for the fish

2 sprigs of fresh thyme

a dash of liquid smoke

3½ ounces trompette mushrooms, washed

1¼ cups Chicken Stock (see page 216)

1 sprig of fresh parsley, finely chopped

**To garnish**

2 Jerusalem artichokes, cut into paper-thin slices

Heat the vegetable oil to 350°F in a deep-fat fryer, or in a deep heavy saucepan.

Put the artichokes and salsify into a saucepan, cover with cold water, and add salt and a squeeze of lemon juice to help keep them nice and white. Bring to a boil, then lower the heat and simmer gently until a knife goes through with a little resistance.

Carefully lower the sliced artichokes for the garnish into the hot oil in batches, and deep-fry for 1 to 2 minutes, or until golden brown like potato chips. Remove, drain on paper towels, and season with salt and pepper.

Preheat your oven to 350°F.

Heat a little olive oil in a skillet. Season the monkfish, add to the pan, and cook on both sides to seal. Place the pieces of fish on a baking pan lined with nonstick parchment paper and put a small pat of butter and a sprig of thyme on top of each one. Place in the oven for about 10 to 15 minutes, or until cooked through.

Allow the remaining stick of butter to soften, and then beat in the liquid smoke until you have the desired taste, mixing well. Put into the fridge to firm up a little.

Melt the smoked butter in a skillet, then add the artichokes, salsify, and mushrooms and sauté until caramelized. Gradually add the chicken stock, allowing it to reduce after each addition to create a rich butter sauce around the vegetables. This should take about 10 minutes. Season with salt and pepper and stir in the chopped parsley.

After 15 minutes the fish should be ready. Remove from the oven and let it rest for 5 minutes. Place the vegetables in a bowl with the fish sitting on top and the Jerusalem artichoke chips sprinkled around.

Tom came up with this idea, and it's typical of his style: fresh, simple, and downright tasty. Mackerel, when fresh out of the water, is hard to beat. Such beautiful colors in the skin, and the deep, earthy flavor goes really well with the smoky bacon and fresh minted peas.

# Cornish Mackerel with Split Peas, Mint, and Bacon

**Serves:** 2

**Preparation time:** 30 minutes, plus soaking

**Cooking time:** 1½ hours

½ cup split green peas (follow package instructions for soaking)

½ an onion, left in one piece

1 small stalk of celery

1 bay leaf

1 sprig of fresh thyme

1½ to 2 cups Chicken Stock (see page 216)

sea salt and freshly ground black pepper

4 strips of smoked bacon, cut into ½-inch lardons

2 slices of sourdough bread, cut into ½-inch dice

olive oil, for frying

4 fresh mackerel fillets, boned

6 fresh mint leaves, roughly chopped

2 handfuls of pea shoots

2 tablespoons Sherry Dressing (see page 216)

First, drain your soaked peas. Give them a good wash and put them into a medium saucepan. Add the onion, celery, bay leaf, and thyme, and enough chicken stock to cover. Season with salt and pepper, bring to a boil, then lower the heat and cook gently at a simmer, using the rest of the chicken stock to top it off as necessary—they should be cooked in about 45 to 50 minutes.

Put the bacon into a skillet over medium heat and cook to release the fat. When the bacon starts to color, add the diced bread and let it fry in the bacon fat until it becomes crunchy. Set aside if not using immediately.

When ready to serve, heat another skillet and add a drizzle of olive oil. Season the mackerel fillets on both sides and add them to the pan, skin-side down. They may contract a little, but don't worry, just gently press them back down for a few seconds and they will relax back to normal. Sear over medium heat for about 4 minutes, or until crisp and golden brown. At this point they will almost be cooked through, but turn each one over and allow the flesh to finish cooking through.

Fold the mint into the split peas and place in the bottom of each serving bowl. Put the mackerel fillets on top, then a good spoonful of the bacon and bread mixture. Finally, garnish with the pea shoots, dressed with the sherry dressing.

Serves: 4

Preparation time: 1 hour

Cooking time: 2 hours

### For the sage and onion stuffing

1 stick butter

1 onion, minced

1 garlic clove, minced

sea salt and freshly ground black pepper

2 sprigs of fresh sage

1 handful of mixed wild mushrooms, roughly chopped

4¼ ounces sourdough bread, crusts removed, cut into ½-inch dice

1 handful of ready-cooked chestnuts, crushed

2 eggs

3 Cumberland or other high-quality pork sausages, casing removed

### For the chicken

1 large plump whole chicken, organic or free-range

1 onion, peeled and halved

1 head of garlic, halved horizontally

2 sprigs of fresh thyme

1 sprig of fresh rosemary

1 sprig of fresh sage, finely chopped

olive oil

2 pints Chicken Stock (see page 216)

### For the roast potatoes

3 tablespoons duck fat

8 round red potatoes, peeled and halved

1 sprig of fresh rosemary

1 sprig of fresh thyme

3 garlic cloves, unpeeled

### For the chicken skin gravy

3½ ounces chicken skins

olive oil

2 shallots, sliced

1 sprig of fresh thyme

It goes without saying that a Sunday roast is my all-time favorite meal. Whether it's after soccer as a kid, or after a long week at work, nothing can soothe your pains like a good roast. It's something every family should do on a Sunday—invite friends, colleagues, whoever, just roast some meat and eat it together, with enough roasted vegetables to induce a food coma. Use whatever vegetables are in season: parsnips and collard greens, mashed turnips, sprouting broccoli, buttered carrots—the list goes on.

# Sunday Chicken

First, make the stuffing. Melt the butter in a skillet and cook the onion and garlic until soft. Season with salt and pepper. Add the sage and the mushrooms, and continue to cook until soft and translucent. Add the bread and let it soak up any butter, then transfer to a mixing bowl. Add the chestnuts and give it all a good stir. Let cool, then add the eggs and sausage meat and stir well. Set aside in the fridge.

Preheat your oven to 350°F. Make sure all the guts are removed from the chicken and fill the cavity with the stuffing. If there's any stuffing left over, you can either freeze it for next time, or roll it into balls and bake it separately.

Put the onion, garlic, and herbs into a roasting pan. Place the chicken on top, and drizzle with olive oil. Season well and place in the oven. After about 40 minutes the chicken will be nice and brown—at this point add half the stock, then lower the oven temperature to 320°F and roast for a further 30 minutes, or until cooked.

In the meantime, make your roast potatoes. Place the duck fat in a roasting pan and put it into the oven. Put the potatoes into a saucepan and cover with cold water. Season really well—don't be shy with the salt. Bring the potatoes to a boil, then lower the heat and let simmer gently until they are halfway cooked. Strain, and let them sit on the side on a tray or plate. Don't shake them, just let the steam escape.

Take the pan of hot duck fat out of the oven and carefully add the potatoes, taking care not to cause the fat to splash, or you'll burn yourself. Using a spoon, baste each potato with the fat, then put them into the oven. Keep basting every 20 minutes or so, and after the first 30 minutes add the rosemary, thyme, and garlic. They should be ready in 1½ hours.

To make the gravy, put the chicken skins into a saucepan with a splash of olive oil over medium heat and cook gently, stirring frequently, until they begin to color. Don't worry if they catch a little, just keep scraping the pan (that's where all the flavor is). As the fat is released, pour it away. Once nicely colored and the fat has been released, add the shallots and thyme, and cook for a further 10 minutes or so.

When the chicken is ready, take it out of the oven and let it rest for about 30 minutes. Strain the stock from the pan and add to the pan of chicken skin. Add the rest of the stock and turn the heat up high. Reduce rapidly for about 20 minutes, or until you have a gravy consistency. Strain and serve alongside your chicken, carving at the table.

Serves: 4

**Preparation time:** 1 day

**Cooking time:** 3 hours, 40 minutes

4 duck legs

3½ ounces Duck Cure
(see page 218)

2½ cups duck fat, enough to
cover the duck legs

oil, for brushing

butter, for frying

4 duck eggs

**For the waffle mix**

1½ cups all-purpose flour

1 tablespoon superfine sugar

1 teaspoon baking powder

½ teaspoon baking soda

a pinch of salt

¾ cup buttermilk

2½ tablespoons butter, melted

1 small egg

**For the maple syrup**

scant 1 cup maple syrup

2½ tablespoons yellow mustard seeds

1 teaspoon mustard powder

1-inch piece of cinnamon stick

1 sprig of fresh thyme

You will also need a waffle iron

Timon Balloo, Executive Chef and Partner at Duck & Waffle's sister restaurant Sugarcane, in Midtown Miami, created this iconic dish and explains how this dish was born: "This dish encompasses my upbringing in urban California, eating fried chicken and waffles, and my refined culinary training working with some great French chefs. And the egg part? If I had my way I'd put eggs on top of everything. But in this case it works especially well when you burst the yolk and it oozes into the meat; add a little of the mustard seed maple syrup and it's an awesome balance of sweet and savory."

# Duck and Waffle with Mustard Maple Syrup

The day before, sprinkle the duck legs all over with the cure. Put them into a container with a lid and leave in the fridge overnight.

The next day, preheat your oven to 285°F. Take out the duck legs and brush off all of the cure. Place in a baking dish and cover with the duck fat. Put into the oven and cook for approximately 3 hours, or until the meat just falls off the bone. Let the duck legs cool in the fat.

To make the waffle mixture, put the flour, sugar, baking powder, baking soda, and salt into a bowl and whisk together. In another bowl, whisk together the buttermilk, melted butter, and egg, then beat this into the flour mixture until just combined. The batter will be quite thick, which is perfectly normal. Put into the fridge until you are ready to make your waffles.

Combine all the ingredients for the maple syrup in a saucepan and bring to a boil. Take off the heat and let cool so the flavors can infuse. Remove the cinnamon and thyme, but leave the mustard seeds, as they add a nice dimension when bitten into.

When ready to serve, preheat your oven to 350°F and turn on your waffle iron. Heat an ovenproof skillet and add the duck legs, skin-side down. Once the skin starts to crisp, turn the legs over and put into the oven for about 8 to 10 minutes, or until crisp.

While the duck legs are in the oven, make your 4 waffles. Brush the hot waffle iron with oil and pour a ladle of batter into each mold. Spread it all around, as the batter is quite thick and won't spread on its own. Cook for about 3 minutes, or until golden and cooked through.

Put another skillet on to heat. Melt some butter in the hot skillet and gently fry the duck eggs, spooning the hot butter over the yolk right at the end.

Serve a duck leg on top of each waffle, with an egg on top of the duck, and maple syrup on the side. When eating, crack the yolk first, then pour the syrup over it, otherwise the syrup tends to slip off the egg.

Nothing says "for the table" more than a whole roasted ham hock studded with aromatic cloves and glazed with honey. I love to serve this simply with whatever vegetables are at the market, and with freshly baked bread and loads of butter, but you can try serving it with mashed potatoes or even a root vegetable gratin. In this recipe we use the colorful heirloom carrots and an interesting technique of baking turnips in salt. Make sure you save the stock from cooking the ham—it's great in soups and stews for that smoked bacon hit.

# Honey-glazed Ham Hock with Carrots and Salt-baked Turnips

**Serves:** 2 to 3

**Preparation time:** 1 hour

**Cooking time:** 5 hours

1 smoked ham hock

1 onion, halved

1 stalk of celery

2 carrots, halved

1 bay leaf

1 sprig of fresh thyme

10 black peppercorns

8 cloves

2 turnips, peeled

2 tablespoons honey

½ stick butter

6 heirloom carrots, blanched (left whole)

sprig of fresh thyme (optional)

1 good handful of watercress

3 tablespoons Sherry Dressing (see page 216)

**For the salt crust**

2 cups all-purpose flour

¾ cup sea salt

½ cup + 2 tablespoons water

Put the ham hock, onion, celery, carrots, bay leaf, thyme, and peppercorns into a large saucepan and cover with cold water. Bring to a boil, then lower the heat and let simmer for approximately 3 to 3½ hours, or until the meat comes away from the bone. Make sure you skim all the time, and top off with water when necessary. Let the ham cool in the stock, then take out and carefully peel away the leathery skin. Score the fat and evenly stud with the cloves, then place in a baking dish. Reserve the stock.

Preheat your oven to 350°F.

To make the salt dough, mix the flour and salt in a bowl, and add the water until you have a firm dough. You may not need to use all the water. Divide in half, then wrap each turnip in the dough so it's totally encased. Arrange them on a roasting pan.

Pour 3 tablespoons of the ham stock around the ham hock, then drizzle the honey over the ham and place in the bottom of the oven. Place the turnips in the oven on the middle rack. Both should take around 30 minutes if the ham hock was at room temperature or hotter. (If you cooked it in advance and refrigerated it, start the hock in the oven 45 minutes before the turnips, at 320°F, then when you add the turnips increase the heat to 350°F. This will give the hock a nice glaze, but keep an eye on it.) Baste the hock with any honey that runs off.

While the ham and turnips are cooking, melt the butter in a skillet and add your carrots. Slowly cook them so they begin to color and the butter foams. Feel free to add a sprig of thyme here, if you like.

When the hock and turnips are ready, remove them both from the oven. Carefully break off the salt crust from the turnips and discard. Slice the turnips about ¼ inch thick.

Put the hock, carrots, and turnips on a large serving plate, and pour any juice from the ham hock all over and around. Serve with the watercress dressed with the sherry dressing.

**Serves:** 8 to 10

**Preparation time:** 30 minutes, plus soaking

**Cooking time:** 6 hours

1 cooked ham hock (cooked according to the recipe for the ham hock opposite, up to the stage where you remove the skin, stock reserved and strained)

**For the stuffing**

½ stick butter

3 tablespoons olive oil

2 onions, minced

2 stalks of celery, finely diced

2 garlic cloves, minced

6 fresh sage leaves, coarsely sliced

1 handful of mixed wild mushrooms, cut into ¾-inch pieces

1½ cups pearl barley (see package instructions for soaking)

ham stock (from cooking the ham) or chicken stock

3 handfuls of ham hock meat, picked to small pieces

**For the suckling pig**

1 suckling pig, boned, head left on

3 apples, halved

2 onions, halved

3 carrots, halved

2 cups apple juice

2 cups Chicken Stock (see page 216)

1 scant cup maple syrup, divided

½ stick butter

**To garnish**

watercress

mixed pickles (apple, carrot, fennel, and/or turnip, see page 216)

This is a real showstopper, a dish created by one of our sous chefs, Jacek. Get it cooking in the early afternoon and your house will be full of the wonderful aromas of suckling pig by the time your friends or family arrive. If you make pickles, make a varied batch so you always have some on hand, using the pickling liquid on page 216. Pickled apple, carrot, fennel, and turnip all work well with this, but pretty much anything goes. The idea is to have some acidity to cut the richness.

# Slow-roasted Suckling Pig with Mushrooms and Barley

First make the stuffing. Heat the butter and oil in a Dutch oven, then add the onion, celery, garlic, sage, and mushrooms and cook gently until soft and tender. Drain the soaked barley and add to the pot, stirring to give it a good coating of butter and oil. Add enough of the ham stock to cover (or chicken stock if you don't have ham stock), bring to a boil, then reduce the heat and simmer. Continue to cook and add stock when needed for about 45 minutes, or until the barley is soft and looks like a loose risotto. Mix in the ham hock meat and set aside to cool.

Preheat your oven to 250°F.

Open out the suckling pig and place the stuffing in the stomach cavity. Roll up and tie with kitchen string.

Put the halved apples, onions, and carrots into a large roasting pan and set the suckling pig on top, bent slightly so it fits snugly, without it touching the pan. Add the apple juice and chicken stock, then cover the whole dish with foil. You may want to cover the ears with an extra layer of foil to avoid burning. Roast in the oven for approximately 4 hours, or until the meat is tender and the skin is soft and sticky.

Gently transfer the suckling pig from the pan into another clean one, and turn the oven up to 320°F. Pour one-third of the maple syrup evenly over the pig and place in the oven. After 20 minutes, pour over half the remaining maple syrup, and pour over the rest after a further 20 minutes for one last glaze.

In the meantime, strain the roasting juices from the first pan into a saucepan (discard the apples, onions, and carrots), bring to a boil, then reduce the heat and simmer until reduced by half. Add the butter to enrich the gravy, swirling the pan around to emulsify it.

Serve a good slice of suckling pig on each plate with some of the gravy poured onto it, garnished with watercress and pickled vegetables.

Vignole is a wonderful thing: a glorious green stew of artichokes, peas, and fava beans enriched with lardo, and it's perfect with slow-braised pork belly melting within it. At the restaurant, we cook the pork belly for 15 hours in a water bath, but the recipe below has been adapted for home cooking.

# Slow-braised Pork Belly with Vignole

**Serves:** 4

**Preparation time:** 30 minutes

**Cooking time:** 2 hours

piece of pork belly, weighing 1 pound 5 ounces, cut into 4 equal slices, approximately 1 inch thick

sea salt and freshly ground black pepper

olive oil

4 slices of lardo, sliced paper-thin

1 onion, thinly sliced

2 garlic cloves, crushed

1 sprig of fresh thyme

1 bay leaf

1 glass of white wine

2 cups Chicken Stock (see page 216)

4 violet artichokes, left whole, stems trimmed to 1 ¼ inches

1 handful of shelled peas, blanched and refreshed

1 handful of shelled fava beans, blanched and refreshed

¾ stick butter

1 sprig of fresh mint, finely chopped

Season the slices of pork with salt and pepper, then heat some olive oil in a Dutch oven and seal the slices on both sides until golden. Remove and set aside.

Add the lardo, onion, garlic, thyme, and bay leaf to the pot and cook really slowly, with no color. Add the wine and cook until reduced by half, then put the pork back in and add the chicken stock. Cover and let simmer for approximately 1 hour, or until tender.

Meanwhile, boil the artichokes for 10 to 12 minutes, or until tender, then drain and refresh in cold water. Drain again, then remove and discard the outer leaves and the furry choke and cut into quarters.

Remove the cooked pork from the Dutch oven and set aside. Add the peas, fava beans, and artichokes to the stock and season again if necessary. Bring to a boil, then lower the heat and simmer for 10 minutes. Add the butter and stir it in to enrich the stock.

Add the mint, then return the pork to the Dutch oven. Let sit for 5 minutes, then serve in bowls, finished with a drizzle of olive oil.

**Serves:** 4

**Preparation time:** 20 minutes

**Cooking time:** 2 hours

olive oil

2 onions, finely sliced

2 cups Chicken Stock (see page 216), simmered until concentrated and reduced by half

2 tablespoons wholegrain mustard

2 sprigs of fresh parsley, chopped

**For the faggots**

7 ounces ground mutton shoulder

3½ ounces ground mutton liver

2 ground mutton kidneys

7 ounces ground bacon

1⅔ cups bread crumbs

1 onion, minced and cooked gently with no color

½ teaspoon ground mace

½ teaspoon ground allspice

1 sprig of fresh rosemary, finely chopped

sea salt and freshly ground black pepper

caul fat, to wrap

**For the beet and celeriac relish**

olive oil

1 teaspoon yellow mustard seeds

1 teaspoon onion seeds

1 sprig of fresh rosemary

7 ounces beets, roasted and finely chopped

7 ounces celeriac, finely diced and blanched

1 onion, minced

¼ cup superfine sugar

3 tablespoons water

3 tablespoons cider vinegar

seeds of 2 cardamom pods

Faggots are an old British classic that should be cooked more at home. We make them with mutton, to help with the mutton renaissance, but you can easily swap the meat for pork. Make sure you have lots of crusty bread on hand or, failing that, a good scoop of mashed potatoes.

# Mutton Faggots with Beet and Celeriac Relish

First, make the faggots. Put all the faggot ingredients, except the caul, into a bowl, mix well, and season with salt and pepper. Shape the mixture into golfball-size balls and wrap them in the caul, ensuring it goes all the way around. Put them on a plate and place in the fridge until you need them.

Next, make the relish. Heat a splash of olive oil in a medium saucepan, add the mustard seeds, onion seeds, and rosemary, and cook gently with no color for about 5 minutes. The seeds may pop, so have a lid handy. Add all the other relish ingredients and cook gently for approximately 30 minutes, or until it has reduced to a chutney-like consistency.

Heat a little olive oil in another medium saucepan, add the sliced onions, and cook slowly until a deep golden color. Add the faggots and gently seal, taking care not to burn the onions.

Now add the stock and gently simmer for 20 minutes. Add the mustard, give it a good stir, and finish with the chopped parsley. Serve with plenty of relish and lots of crusty bread.

**Serves:** 4

**Preparation time:** 1 hour, plus chilling and cooling

**Cooking time:** 2 hours

**For the ragout**

olive oil

3 rabbit legs, on the bone

2 slices of pancetta, finely diced

2 shallots, minced

2 stalks of celery, finely diced

3 garlic cloves, minced

3 sprigs of fresh rosemary, leaves picked and finely chopped

3 sprigs of fresh sage, leaves picked and finely chopped

1 glass of white wine

4¼ pints Chicken Stock (see page 216)

sea salt and freshly grated black pepper

½ cup grated Parmesan cheese

**For the pasta**

4 cups "OO" pasta flour

5 large eggs

all-purpose flour, for dusting

semolina, for dusting

**To garnish**

½ stick butter

8 fresh sage leaves

aged pecorino cheese, or Parmesan

You will also need a pasta machine

The River Café in London is one of my favorite restaurants. It's an example of what a restaurant should be, and indeed how food should be: the finest ingredients cooked with love, care, and attention in a warm and friendly environment. Before we opened Duck & Waffle I spent a day in their kitchen, and this is a version of one of the dishes I learned that day—I was drawn to the pasta station almost immediately.

# Rabbit Agnoli with Sage Brown Butter

First, make the rabbit ragout. Heat a little olive oil in a medium saucepan, then add the rabbit legs and brown them on all sides. Take out and place on a plate, then add the pancetta, shallots, celery, garlic, rosemary, and sage to the pan and cook gently for 8 to 10 minutes, but with no color. Put the rabbit legs back into the pan, add the wine, and simmer until reduced by half. Add enough chicken stock to cover, season with salt and pepper, then lower the heat and simmer slowly for about 1½ hours, or until the meat comes away from the bone easily.

Next, make the pasta. Add the flour and eggs to a mixing bowl and mix together well, kneading until smooth. Cover the bowl with plastic wrap and put in the fridge.

When the rabbit legs are ready, take them out of the pan and set aside. Discard all but 2 cups of the stock and simmer it until reduced by three-quarters. When the rabbit is cool enough to handle, flake it into tiny pieces, or finely chop, and put back into the pan. Mix really well, and if there is any liquid remaining, cook until it has evaporated but not totally dried out. Let cool, then stir in the Parmesan and set aside.

Using a pasta machine, roll out your pasta gradually, starting from the thickest setting down to the thinnest. Fold the pasta back together and repeat. It should be super stretchy. Lay out the pasta on a floured surface, and on one half of the sheet put grape-size balls of the rabbit mixture, allowing 1½ inches free all around. You should be able to make 24 agnoli (6 per person) from this amount of pasta. Run your finger, dipped in cold water, around the sides of the filling, then fold over the other half of the pasta and gently press down so it sticks, avoiding any air. Cut out rectangles, approximately 2½ x 1½ inches, between the mounds of filling. Take diagonal opposite corners and pinch them together, to make a small parcel. Store in the fridge, on a baking pan dusted with semolina.

When ready to cook, bring a large saucepan of salted water to a boil and cook your agnoli for 3 minutes.

Heat the butter and sage leaves in a separate saucepan and let them foam. When the leaves are crisp, remove with a slotted spoon, drain on paper towels, and reserve. Strain the pasta and add to the pan of foaming butter. Let the butter brown a little, then transfer the pasta to serving plates. Add a good grating of aged pecorino, a drizzle of the brown butter, the crispy sage leaves, and a touch of olive oil to finish.

This is my favorite pasta dish from our restaurant menu and has been the best received, using the finest of winter vegetables—Jerusalem artichokes. Making pasta is so rewarding and relaxing, and every time you make it you learn so much and see yourself improve. Once you feel comfortable, experiment with various shapes.

# Jerusalem Artichoke and Truffle Ravioli

**Serves:** 6 (5 ravioli per person)

**Preparation time:** 1 ½ hours, plus chilling

**Cooking time:** 30 minutes

### For the pasta

4 cups "OO" pasta flour

5 large eggs

all-purpose flour, for dusting

semolina, for dusting

### For the filling

olive oil

1 pound 2 ounces Jerusalem artichokes, peeled and cut into 1-inch pieces

scant 1 cup heavy cream

½ cup finely grated Parmesan cheese

sea salt and freshly ground black pepper

¾-ounce truffle (fresh if possible, or slices in oil), finely chopped

### To finish

½ stick butter

10 turnip leaves, finely chopped

scant ½ cup hazelnuts, roasted and crushed

aged pecorino cheese, or Parmesan, grated just before cooking

You will also need a pasta machine

First, make the pasta. Put the flour and eggs into a bowl and mix together really well, kneading until smooth. Cover with plastic wrap and put into the fridge for 30 minutes.

Now make the filling. Heat a little olive oil in a medium saucepan and cook the artichokes gently for 8 minutes. Add the cream and reduce the heat. Let the artichokes simmer until soft, at which point use a slotted spoon to remove them from the cream, put them into a food processor, and blitz until smooth. If the mixture is too thick, add a little of the cream from the pan. Let the purée cool, then add the Parmesan, salt, pepper, and truffle.

Using a pasta machine, roll out your pasta gradually, starting from the thickest setting down to the thinnest it will go. Fold the pasta back together and repeat. It should be super stretchy. Lay out the pasta on a floured surface, and on one half of the sheet put grape-size dollops of the artichoke purée, allowing 1 ¼ inches free all around. You should be able to make 30 ravioli from this amount of pasta. Run your finger, dipped in cold water, around the sides of the filling, then fold over the other half of the pasta and gently press down so that it sticks, avoiding any air. Cut out the ravioli between the mounds of filling with a cookie cutter, one that allows a rim of ¾ inch to 1 ¼ inches around the filling (a 2 ½-inch cookie cutter should do). Store in the fridge, on a baking pan dusted with semolina.

When ready to cook, bring a large saucepan of salted water to a boil and cook your ravioli for 3 minutes.

In another saucepan, melt the butter and gently cook the turnip leaves for 2 minutes, or until just wilted. Using a slotted spoon, remove the ravioli from the water and add to the butter and turnip leaves. Add a tablespoon of the pasta water and let it bubble so that the sauce emulsifies. Keep the pasta moving at all times to stop them from frying like dumplings.

Turn out onto a serving dish and garnish with the crushed hazelnuts and freshly grated pecorino (or Parmesan).

DESSERTS

**Serves:** 12

**Preparation time:** 2 days (if making it all from scratch)

**Cooking time:** 30 minutes

14-ounce can of condensed milk

1 handful of Honeycomb (see page 219), crushed into ½-inch pieces

**For the peanut butter ice cream**

2 cups milk

2 cups heavy cream

1 vanilla bean

scant 1 cup superfine sugar

¼ cup smooth peanut butter

10 egg yolks

**For the marshmallow**

3½ tablespoons light corn syrup

scant ¼ cup superfine sugar

1½ tablespoons water

1 egg white

a small pinch of salt

**For the brownie**

10 ounces baking chocolate (70% cocoa)

2½ sticks unsalted butter

2 cups superfine sugar

6 eggs

heaping 1 cup all-purpose flour, sifted

¾ cup unsweetened cocoa powder, sifted

6 ounces white chocolate chunks

You will also need a candy thermometer

This is a dish, that in one form or another, has been on the restaurant menu since we opened. I know every chef and home cook alike states that they have the greatest brownie recipe ever, but, believe me, look no further. It's here. It has now evolved into a sundae, which you can do too by simply layering the various elements in a tall glass. If you have any caramelized nuts lying around, they make a great addition. Hazelnuts, almonds, or peanuts all work perfectly, as does a dollop of Chantilly cream on the top.

# Brownies with Peanut Butter Ice Cream and Marshmallow

### DAY 1

First, place the unopened can of condensed milk in a saucepan and cover with water. Bring to a boil, then lower the heat and simmer for 4 hours, making sure you top off the water throughout so that the can is always submerged. Let cool. When cool, open the can—a caramel will have formed. Spoon out into a bowl, cover with plastic wrap, and leave in the fridge until ready to use.

To make the ice cream, bring the milk, cream, and vanilla to a boil in a large saucepan. Meanwhile, put the sugar, peanut butter, and egg yolks into a bowl and whisk very well. (Sugar absorbs moisture, and if you don't mix right away you will have pieces of dried egg yolk where all the moisture has been removed by the sugar, so beware.)

Once the milk and cream mixture comes to a boil, pour half onto the yolk mix and whisk together. Pour this back into the remaining milk and cream in the saucepan and heat gently until thickened. In the kitchen we use a candy thermometer to check once it is cooked—183°F is the temperature we take it to (any higher and the egg will scramble, leaving your ice cream lumpy)—but if you don't have a thermometer, cook until the mixture coats the back of a wooden spoon and stays there without running right off. Strain the mixture, transfer to another bowl to stop it from cooking, then let cool and churn.

If you don't have an ice-cream machine, freeze the mixture in four batches and, once frozen, blend in a food processor. Return to the freezer after blending.

If you don't have honeycomb on hand, now's the time to make it (see page 219).

To make the marshmallow, place the light corn syrup, sugar, and water in a saucepan and, over medium heat, cook to 242°F on a candy thermometer. In the meantime, whisk the egg white and salt together until fluffy. Slowly add the syrup mixture, the same as when making Italian meringue (see page 160), and continue whisking until the mixture is thick and the bowl has cooled. Spoon out into a container and store in the fridge.

Continued over the page

## DAY 2

Now make your brownie. Preheat your oven to 350°F, and line a 14 x 10-inch baking pan with nonstick parchment paper.

Put the chocolate and butter into a heatproof bowl and set it over a saucepan of gently simmering water until melted. In a mixing bowl, beat the sugar and eggs together until light and fluffy. Add the chocolate mixture to the egg mixture and fold in, then fold in the sifted flour and cocoa powder. Fold in the white chocolate and add the batter to the prepared baking pan. Place in the oven and bake for 20 minutes. It may look undercooked when you take it out, but when it's cooled it will be perfect and soft.

To serve, there are no real rules. At the restaurant, we spread the marshmallow over the bottom of the plate and blowtorch it to give it a nice toasty taste. Then we simply cut the brownie into squares (they don't have to be perfect), and serve with a good scoop of ice cream, some crumbled honeycomb, and a spoonful of the dulce de leche caramel.

This is what Tom does when he's hungry and hung over; he makes kickass desserts. It started off as a cure, then became one of our best-selling dessert specials to date. If it's on the board, you know someone's feeling tender.

# Cherry Cola Float

**Makes:** 2

**Preparation time:** 10 minutes

**Cooking time:** none

2 scoops of Vanilla Ice Cream (see page 219)

²/₃ cup pitted cherries

½ a can of cola

1½ tablespoons grenadine

Put a scoop of ice cream into the bottom of each sundae glass, or use bowls if you don't have those.

Divide the cherries between the glasses, then pour in the cola, one-quarter of a can per glass. Drizzle with the grenadine to finish.

This is one of my all-time favorite desserts. It requires a bit of preparation, but once the elements are done, it's relatively straightforward to make and have ready in the freezer for whenever you need to wow your friends. The toasty meringue reminds me of marshmallows charred on the fire, and the cold ice cream complements it perfectly.

# Baked Alaska with Strawberry Juice

**Serves:** 6

**Preparation time:** 1 hour, plus cooling, chilling, and freezing

**Cooking time:** 1 hour

6 balls of Vanilla Ice Cream (see page 219), frozen hard

**For the dulce de leche sponge cake**

⅔ stick unsalted butter, softened, plus extra for greasing

1½ tablespoons light corn syrup

14-ounce can of dulce de leche (milk caramel)

2 eggs

heaping ¾ cup all-purpose flour sifted with 1 teaspoon baking powder

**For the strawberry juice**

2 cups strawberries

⅓ cup strawberry liqueur (or another fruity liqueur, or rum)

1 tablespoon superfine sugar

**For the Italian meringue**

1 cup + 2 tablespoons superfine sugar

½ cup + 2 tablespoons water

3¼ ounces egg whites

You will also need a candy thermometer and a pastry bag with a plain ⅜-inch tip

Preheat the oven to 350°F. Lightly grease a 12-inch lipped baking pan and cover with nonstick parchment paper.

To make the sponge cake, put the softened butter, light corn syrup, and dulce de leche (milk caramel) into a mixing bowl and, using an electric stand mixer, or a wooden spoon if doing by hand, cream together until lighter in color—this should take about 5 minutes. Crack the eggs into a bowl and whisk together. Still creaming the butter mixture, add the eggs, then mix together for another 2 minutes, or until completely smooth. Sift in the flour and mix for 1 more minute. Spoon your batter onto the prepared baking pan and spread out until it is ½ inch thick. Bake in the oven for 8 to 10 minutes, then transfer to a rack to cool. Using a cookie cutter with a 4-inch diameter, cut out 6 disks of sponge cake and set aside.

To make the strawberry juice, wash and hull the strawberries, then cut them in half or quarters if large. Place in a metal bowl, add the liqueur and sugar, cover tightly with plastic wrap, and place over a saucepan of simmering water, making sure the bottom of the bowl doesn't touch the water. Let simmer for 30 minutes, then remove from the heat. Once cooled a little, strain off and discard the pulp. Place the liquid in the fridge to chill.

To make the meringue, put the sugar into a small saucepan over low heat and gently add the water. Make sure no sugar has come up the sides of the pan, as this will make the syrup crystallize. Put the egg whites into a mixing bowl and, using an electric stand mixer, beat on slow speed. Once the sugar has reached 240°F, increase the speed of beating to create soft peaks. When the sugar has reached 250°F, pour it slowly onto the egg whites while still beating on a high speed. Once the sugar syrup has been added, continue to beat until the meringue has cooled to room temperature, then put into a pastry bag with a plain ⅜-inch tip.

To finish, put the sponge cake disks on individual pieces of nonstick parchment paper arranged on a cookie sheet and place a ball of ice cream on each disk. Pipe the meringue all the way around, to completely cover. At this stage place in the freezer until you are ready to cook and serve.

When ready to cook, preheat your oven to 400°F. Place the cookie sheet on the bottom shelf for 3 minutes, or until the meringue is nicely browned. Carefully transfer to serving bowls and pour the strawberry juice around each one.

If a Sunday roast were part of my last meal on this planet, then a steamed pudding would have to be the dessert. The classic British dessert combination of treacle sponge with custard is divine, but at the restaurant we add some wintry orange notes to the dish. Restaurants in England often offer custard or ice cream with puddings; try both. I certainly wouldn't blame you if you did. It's exactly what I do.

# Steamed Orange Puddings with Grand Marnier Custard

**Serves:** 6
**Preparation time:** 30 minutes
**Cooking time:** 1 hour 20 minutes

1⅔ sticks unsalted butter, softened, plus extra for greasing
scant 1 cup superfine sugar
2 oranges
3 eggs
heaping 1 cup all-purpose flour
1 tablespoon baking powder
1⅔ cups bread crumbs

**For the orange syrup**
heaping ¾ cup superfine sugar
2 pints orange juice

**For the Grand Marnier custard**
1 cup milk
1 cup heavy cream
3 egg yolks
scant ¼ cup superfine sugar
2 tablespoons Grand Marnier

Grease six 3½-inch dariole molds with butter and set aside.

To make the puddings, cream the butter and sugar in an electric stand mixer until light in color. Meanwhile, zest both oranges but only juice 1 of them. Add the juice and zest to the bowl once the butter and sugar have creamed, then beat again and add the eggs. Continue to beat, making sure to scrape down the sides. The mixture will split, but don't worry, it will come back together. Now add the flour, baking powder, and bread crumbs and make sure it's really well combined.

Spoon the batter into the molds, filling them two-thirds full, leaving ½ inch free at the top. Cover with foil and use elastic bands or string to hold the foil in place.

Place in a steamer over medium heat, so that there is lots of steam, for 40 minutes.

While the puddings are cooking, make the syrup and custard.

To make the syrup, put the sugar and orange juice into a saucepan and bring to a boil. Continually skimming off any foam, cook the mixture until it has reduced to about 1 scant cup.

To make the custard, heat the milk and cream in a saucepan. Meanwhile, put the egg yolks, sugar, and Grand Marnier into a bowl and whisk together. Once the milk and cream mixture has boiled, slowly pour it onto the yolk mixture and stir well. Put the mixture into a clean saucepan and heat gently until it thickens a little, taking care not scramble the eggs and make it go lumpy. Pass through a sieve and set aside until the puddings are ready.

To serve, spoon some of the custard into each bowl and add the puddings fresh from the steamer. Finish by drizzling about 2 tablespoons of syrup onto each one.

I love the freshness of this dish, but it is dependent on the quality of the fruit. As the ice cream sits on the hot peaches and runs into the honey, it looks so tempting. Italian fruit, in the peak of the season, is hard to beat. As the seasons change, try the same dish with ripe pears. Plums work really well, too.

# Roasted Peaches with Thyme, Honey, and Saffron Sponge Cake

**Serves:** 4

**Preparation time:** 30 minutes

**Cooking time:** 50 minutes

4 ripe peaches, halved and stones removed

8 small sprigs of fresh thyme

generous ⅓ cup liquid honey

4 scoops of Vanilla Ice Cream (see page 219)

**For the saffron sponge**

½ stick unsalted butter, melted, plus extra for greasing

4 eggs

½ cup + 2 tablespoons superfine sugar

a pinch of saffron

1 cup all-purpose flour

To make the sponge cake, preheat your oven to 350°F. Grease an 11¼ x 8½-inch rectangular cake pan and line it with nonstick parchment paper.

Put the eggs, sugar, and saffron into a bowl and whisk over a saucepan of gently simmering water until light and fluffy. Take off the heat and gently fold in the flour, then add the melted butter. Pour into the prepared pan and bake for approximately 15 to 20 minutes, or until a skewer comes out clean when inserted into the center. When baking, try not to open the door until 15 minutes has passed so as not to disturb the rising. Transfer to a rack to cool.

Place the peaches, cut-side up, in a roasting pan lined with nonstick parchment paper. Place a sprig of thyme on top of each peach half and drizzle with the honey. Roast in the oven for approximately 15 minutes, basting the peaches with the honey every 3 to 4 minutes.

To serve, tear the sponge cake into 4 small cookie-size pieces per person, and add 2 halves of peach per plate. Add a scoop of ice cream and a good drizzle of the thyme honey, using some leaves as well—it's all added flavor.

These are ideal little nibbles to have up your sleeve, whether to indulge a sudden sweet craving or to whip out at the end of a meal. Beats buying chocolates—you'll have worked for your reward!

# Homemade Chocolates and Nibbles

**Makes:** 50 x 1-inch pieces
**Preparation time:** 10 minutes
**Cooking time:** 15 minutes

½ ounce gelatin leaves

oil, for greasing

cornstarch or powdered sugar, for dusting

scant ½ cup water

1 cup sugar

2 tablespoons liquid glucose

2¾ ounces egg whites

heaping ⅓ cup lemon curd

1¼ ounces ready-made meringue nests, broken into small pieces

scant ½ cup powdered sugar

heaping ⅓ cup cornstarch

You will also need a candy thermometer

## LEMON MARSHMALLOWS

Put the gelatin leaves into very cold water to soak and become soft. Grease an 8-inch springform cake pan and dust it lightly with cornstarch or powdered sugar.

Carefully put the water, sugar, and glucose into a saucepan, making sure the sugar does not go up the sides. Bring to a boil and put in a candy thermometer. Once it reaches 240°F, put the egg whites into a mixing bowl and, using an electric stand mixer, start beating. When the sugar reaches 250°F, turn off the heat and finish beating the whites until stiff peaks form.

Now slowly pour the sugar syrup into the whites, beating all the time. Drain the gelatin leaves and add them to the mixture while it is still hot. Beat for 2 minutes, then add the lemon curd and meringue and continue to beat.

When the mixture is cold, stop beating and pour it into the prepared cake pan. Level the top with a wet metal spatula, and put into the fridge for 1 hour to set. Remove and cut to the desired shape.

Sift the powdered sugar and cornstarch together and roll your marshmallows in this until they are well coated (this is to stop the marshmallows from sticking together). Now they are ready to serve.

**Makes:** 7 ounces
**Preparation time:** 5 minutes
**Cooking time:** 20 minutes

1⅓ cup almonds, shelled and skinned

heaping ¼ cup superfine sugar

3 tablespoons water

1¼ cups unsweetened cocoa powder

You will also need a candy thermometer

## COCOA ALMONDS

Preheat your oven to 320°F. Place the almonds on a cookie sheet and roast in the oven for 8 to 10 minutes, or until golden brown.

Put the sugar and water into a saucepan and bring to a boil. Put in a candy thermometer and heat until the sugar has reached 240°F. There is quite a small amount of syrup, so you may have to tilt the pan to be able to get a reading on your thermometer. Do so carefully to avoid burning yourself.

Add the hot nuts and stir vigorously—eventually the sugar will crystallize and leave a fine coating around each nut. Return the pan to low heat and continue to cook until the sugar caramelizes. Once each nut is golden brown, take off the heat and add the cocoa powder. Stir until well coated, then put into a sieve to get rid of excess cocoa. Spread the almonds on a cookie sheet lined with nonstick parchment paper to cool.

**Makes:** 50

**Preparation time:** 30 minutes, plus cooling, chilling and freezing

**Cooking time:** 4¼ hours

14-ounce can of condensed milk

a pinch of sea salt

7 ounces baking chocolate (70% cocoa solids), broken into pieces

## SALTED CARAMEL TRUFFLES

Beware! This is a bit of a messy recipe, so don't be scared of getting your hands dirty!

First, place the unopened can of condensed milk in a large saucepan and cover with water. Bring to a boil, then lower the heat and let simmer for 4 hours, making sure you top off the water throughout so the can is always submerged. Remove the can from the water and let cool for 30 minutes.

When cool, open the can and spoon out the caramel into a bowl. Add the salt and mix well. Chill in the fridge for 30 minutes so it firms up a bit—you'll find it much easier to work with.

Once chilled, use a teaspoon to make balls the size of a small marble and place on a plate. Put into the freezer for 2 hours, or until firm.

Melt the chocolate in a heatproof bowl set over a saucepan of gently simmering water. Line a cookie sheet with nonstick parchment paper. Put on disposable gloves (so as not to make too much mess), and take the balls out of the freezer. Coat your gloves with melted chocolate, roll one ball and place on the prepared cookie sheet. Repeat the process until all the balls are coated. Put into the fridge for about 1 hour to set the chocolate and to allow the caramel to defrost and soften.

Makes: 8
Preparation time: 1 hour
Cooking time: 1 hour

**For the peanut brittle**

1 ⅓ cups unsalted peanuts

heaping ¼ cup superfine sugar

a small pinch of sea salt

**For the Italian meringue**

¾ cup superfine sugar

scant ½ cup water

2¼ ounces egg whites

**For the macaroons**

1½ cups ground almonds

1¼ cups powdered sugar

a pinch of red food coloring powder, or a few drops of liquid coloring

2¼ ounces egg whites

**For the peanut butter mousse**

7 ounces Crème Pâtissière (see page 19)

2 tablespoons smooth peanut butter

2 tablespoons cream cheese

scant ½ cup heavy cream, whipped to soft peaks

**To assemble**

¼ cup raspberry jam, divided

2 bananas

superfine sugar, for sprinkling

2 cups raspberries

You will also need a candy thermometer and a pastry bag fitted with a plain tip

PBJ—peanut butter and jam—is such a classic. What I love most is how it can be interpreted in so many ways. We make it classically as a toasted sandwich for brunch, then offer a more refined dessert option for dinner. Every time I eat this my brain is thinking of other ways to use it, maybe a PBJ doughnut or cheesecake or sundae...

# PBJ Macaroon

To make the brittle, preheat the oven to 320°F. Roast the peanuts for approximately 10 minutes. Once they are roasted, put the sugar and salt into a saucepan and over low heat. Allow to caramelize until dark golden—this will give a better flavor, but don't let it get too dark or it will taste bitter. Add the hot nuts and stir quickly, then, using a metal spoon, place on a sheet of nonstick parchment paper and let cool. Once cold, you can blitz the brittle in a food processor or chop it by hand.

Preheat your oven to 320°F again.

To make the meringue, put the sugar into a saucepan and gently add the water. Make sure no sugar comes up the sides of the pan, as this will make the syrup crystallize.

Put the egg whites into an electric stand mixer and beat on slow speed. Once the sugar has reached 240°F on a candy thermometer, increase the speed of beating to create soft peaks. When the sugar has reached 250°F, pour it slowly onto the whites while still beating on high speed. Once the sugar syrup has been added, continue to beat until it has cooled down to room temperature.

Sift the ground almonds and powdered sugar into a bowl and add the food coloring. Add the egg whites and make a paste, using a wooden spoon or rubber spatula. Now beat in the Italian meringue, using an electric mixer or by hand, until it becomes runnier. To check when it is ready to pipe, spoon a small amount onto a plate. If the peak disappears in 1 minute it is ready.

With a pencil, draw circles with a 4-inch diameter on a sheet of nonstick parchment paper, then turn over so the penciled side is underneath. Place on a cookie sheet. Following the lines you can see through the paper, pipe the mixture in a spiral to fill the space.

Place in the oven for 20 minutes, then remove and let cool.

To make the mousse, whisk the crème pâtissière and peanut butter together, then add the cream cheese and mix well. Fold in the whipped cream and add to a pastry bag.

To assemble, put ½ tablespoon of jam on each macaroon and spread it out.

Cut the banana into ¼-inch slices and sprinkle with superfine sugar. Caramelize using a kitchen blowtorch if you have one, or put on a baking pan and caramelize under the broiler. Place about 8 raspberries around the outside of each macaroon, and put 3 slices of caramelized banana in the center. Carefully pipe the mousse on top, creating a nice peak.

Decorate with one further slice of caramelized banana, and scatter the dessert with the peanut brittle.

Makes: 4
Preparation time: 30 minutes
Cooking time: 25 minutes

oil, for deep-frying

1 bottle of ice-cold beer

heaping 1½ cups all-purpose flour, plus extra for dusting

4 chocolate bars
(I use Milky Way™ bars)

**For the malt ice cream**

2 cups heavy cream

2 cups milk

¼ cup malt extract

seeds from 1 vanilla bean

scant 1 cup superfine sugar

10 egg yolks

**For the oat crunch**

1¼ cups all-purpose flour

1¼ cups rolled oats

1½ sticks unsalted butter

2 tablespoons superfine sugar

2 tablespoons milk

1½ tablespoons honey

You will also need a deep-fat fryer

We tried this out on Burns Night and it went crazy. Naturally it went on the menu, but after a few weeks we had to take it off again. Sounds strange, but we couldn't keep up with the volume: when you have 5 or 6 in the fryer, the temperature drops, as does the standard of the batter. This makes far more oat crunch than you need, so you can either halve the quantities, freeze the dough in sausagelike tubes for later use, or have them with cheese—they're great as an alternative to crackers.

# Deep-fried Chocolate Bar with Malt Ice Cream and Oat Crunch

To make the ice cream, bring the cream, milk, malt extract, and vanilla to a boil in a large saucepan. Meanwhile, put the sugar and egg yolks in a bowl and beat very well. (Sugar absorbs moisture, and if you don't mix right away you will have pieces of dried egg yolk where all the moisture has been removed by the sugar, so beware.)

Once the milk and cream mixture comes to a boil, pour half onto the yolk mixture and beat together. Pour this back into the remaining milk and cream in the pan and heat gently until thickened. In the kitchen we use a thermometer to check when it's ready—183°F is the temperature we take it to (any higher and the egg will scramble, leaving your ice cream lumpy)—but if you don't have one, cook until the mixture coats the back of a wooden spoon and stays there without running right off. Strain the mixture, transfer to another bowl to stop it from cooking, then cool and churn in an ice-cream machine. If you don't have an ice-cream machine, freeze the mixture in four batches and, once frozen, blend in a food processor. Return to the freezer after blending. (Alternatively, you could make a plain vanilla base (see page 219) and just before churning add the malt extract—this saves you making multiple ice creams. If you already have plain vanilla ice cream, you can drizzle it with the extract to get the flavor, too.)

To make the oat crunch, put the flour, oats, butter, and sugar into the mixing bowl of an electric stand mixer fitted with the paddle attachment and set on low speed, or use an electric hand mixer. Put the milk and honey into a small saucepan and heat gently until the honey melts and it becomes one liquid. Once the butter has been rubbed into the flour, oats, and sugar, pour in the milk and honey. As soon as it has combined, stop mixing. Shape the mixture into two long sausages, then seal them in plastic wrap and roll them up tightly. Chill them in the fridge for 2 hours—they are then ready to cut and cook.

Preheat your oven to 350°F and line a baking pan with nonstick parchment paper. Unwrap the oat sausages and use a sharp knife to cut them into ¼-inch slices (a little either way won't matter too much). Arrange them evenly on the prepared baking pan. Bake for 7 to 10 minutes, or until they are a nice golden color. Set aside to cool. (These can be made ahead of time and stored in an airtight container.)

When ready to serve, heat the oil to 350°F in your deep-fat fryer.

Slowly beat the beer into the flour to make a smooth batter with the consistency of thick custard. Remove the wrappers from the candy bars, and dust each one with flour. Coat with the batter and carefully drop into the fryer. Cook for about 3 minutes, or until the batter is crispy.

Drain on paper towels, and serve in a bowl with a good scoop of malt ice cream and a couple of oat crunch cookies crumbled on top.

Cheese and port is a very popular combination, so working on the idea of deep red fruit flavors and cheese, we adapted the Lancashire classic by embedding a piece of blue cheese inside. As the cakes bake, the cheese bubbles away and comes through the slices in the pastry, so that they become beautifully rustic. Try these instead of a cheese board at the end of a meal. Stilton is fine to substitute if you can't get hold of Fourme d'Ambert.

# Fourme d'Ambert Eccles Cakes

**Makes:** 12

**Preparation time:** 20 minutes, plus chilling

**Cooking time:** 20 minutes

2 tablespoons unsalted butter, melted

1 cup soft brown sugar

1 cup less 2 tablespoons currants

½ teaspoon freshly grated nutmeg

¼ teaspoon ground allspice

¼ teaspoon ground cinnamon

finely grated zest and juice of ¼ of an orange

1 pound 2 ounces puff pastry, rolled out into sheets ¼ inch thick

10½ ounces Fourme d'Ambert cheese, cut into 12 x ¾-inch cubes

milk, for glazing

superfine sugar, for dusting

Put the butter, sugar, currants, spices, and orange zest and juice into a bowl and stir well to combine. Take a teaspoon of the mixture and roll it into a ball. Continue until you have 12 balls.

Take the pastry sheets and, using a cookie cutter, cut out disks approximately 4 inches in diameter. Place a cube of cheese in the center of each pastry, then set one of the fruit-mixture balls on top, flattened slightly. Brush the sides of the pastry with milk, then lift them up to enclose the mixture, and seal. Turn them over and place on a baking pan lined with nonstick parchment paper. Place in the fridge to rest for 30 minutes.

Preheat your oven to 350°F. Take the cakes from the fridge, make 3 slashes on the top of each one, and brush with milk. Dust with sugar and bake for approximately 20 minutes, or until golden brown.

Pistachio and rose is such a wonderful combination and one that you'll find in many cuisines, including Turkish and Indian, to name but two. The deep, fresh nutty flavor is subtly complemented by the floral rose—add sweetened cream and fresh summer raspberries and the balance is just perfect. This can be a simple cake to take to work, or a glorious masterpiece with swirls of cream, that becomes a beautiful mess once broken into.

# Pistachio and Olive Oil Cake with Rose-scented Chantilly Cream

**Serves:** 8 to 12
**Preparation time:** 30 minutes
**Cooking time:** 45 to 55 minutes

### For the cake

1 stick unsalted butter, plus extra for greasing

heaping 1½ cups green pistachios

scant ½ cup polenta

scant ½ cup all-purpose flour

1 teaspoon baking powder

grated zest and juice of ½ a lemon

grated zest and juice of ½ an orange

½ cup olive oil

3 eggs

1 cup superfine sugar

### For the rose-scented Chantilly cream

1 cup heavy cream

2½ tablespoons superfine sugar

¼ teaspoon rose water or rose essence

### To decorate

fresh raspberries, about 6 per person

scant ½ cup powdered sugar, for dusting

Preheat your oven to 320°F. Lightly grease a 9-inch springform cake pan.

Put the nuts into a food processor and begin to blend them. When they are nearly all blended, stop the machine, add the polenta, flour, and baking powder, then continue blending until they have a coarsely ground texture. Transfer the mixture to a bowl and add the orange and lemon zest and juice.

Gently warm the butter in a small saucepan. Once melted, add the oil and set aside.

Crack the eggs into a mixing bowl, add the sugar, and beat for 5 minutes (the mixture should double in size, if not more). Add the butter and oil mixture, and once everything is combined stop the machine and fold in your pistachio mixture. Pour the batter into the prepared cake pan and bake for approximately 45 minutes. (It should be nice and golden on top and a skewer, when inserted, should come out clean.) Let cool on a wire rack.

To prepare the Chantilly cream, put the cream and sugar into a bowl. The strength of the rose water or essence that you find will change the recipe dramatically, so it's best to add it by taste, a little at a time. When you have enough rose flavor, stop and beat all of the ingredients together until stiff. Keep in the fridge until ready to serve.

Transfer the cake to a serving plate, spoon the Chantilly cream on top, and decorate with the raspberries. Dust with powdered sugar and serve immediately.

This is such a simple dessert, but we have pimped it with bacon. I've no idea why it works, but it just does. Don't be put off by the bacon—the smoky, salty edge that it gives really complements the rich sweet pudding. Give it a try!

# Chocolate Bread Pudding with Bacon Custard

**Serves:** 8 to 10

**Preparation time:** 30 minutes

**Cooking time:** 1 ½ hours

### For the pudding

1 ½ sticks unsalted butter, plus a little extra for greasing

generous ½ cup heavy cream

3 ½ cups milk

1 ½ ounces milk chocolate, coarsely chopped

1 ½ ounces baking chocolate (70% cocoa), coarsely chopped

4 egg yolks

scant ¾ cup superfine sugar, plus extra for dusting

1 loaf of good-quality white bread, sliced and buttered

powdered sugar, for dusting

### For the custard

6 strips of smoked bacon

½ cup + 2 tablespoons milk

½ cup + 2 tablespoons heavy cream

2 egg yolks

3 tablespoons superfine sugar

Preheat your oven to 285°F and butter a baking dish approximately 11¼ x 9 inches in size.

To make the pudding, put the cream and milk into a saucepan and bring to a boil, then add the chocolate and whisk in until melted. Remove from the heat. Whisk together the yolks and sugar in a bowl, then add them to the chocolate cream. Whisk well, then strain.

Use the butter to butter the bread, then layer it in the dish, with ladles of the chocolate custard in between. Press down with your fingers to make sure all the bread is soaked properly. Dust the top with a few pinches of sugar, and place in the oven for 30 minutes.

In the meantime, make your custard. Put the bacon into a medium saucepan and caramelize over medium heat, pouring away any fat that comes out. When it's all browned, add the milk and cream and bring to a boil. Lower the heat and let the mixture infuse over low heat for 30 minutes.

In a bowl, whisk together the egg yolks and sugar. Bring the cream back to a boil, and strain. Slowly pour the cream into the yolk mixture and stir well. Pour it all back into the pan and heat gently until it thickens a little, taking care not to let it scramble and become lumpy.

Serve the pudding with the custard poured over and around it, dusted lightly with powdered sugar.

What every kid wants, and always a winner. The ice cream reminds me of Mini Milks and takes me straight back to my childhood. As for the freshly baked cookies, who doesn't love them? You can swap the dark chocolate for milk or white, and adding nuts is a great idea, too.

# Cookies and Milk

**Serves:** 8

**Preparation time:** 10 minutes, plus freezing

**Cooking time:** 30 minutes

**For the milk ice cream**

scant 1 cup heavy cream

3½ cups milk, divided

1 cup superfine sugar

8 egg yolks

**For the cookies**

1 stick unsalted butter

¾ cup superfine sugar

1 egg

1 cup dark chocolate chips

1¼ cups all-purpose flour

¼ teaspoon baking powder

To make the milk ice cream, put the cream into a saucepan with a generous 2½ cups of the milk and heat to just below boiling. While this is heating, put the sugar and egg yolks into a bowl and whisk very well. (Sugar absorbs moisture, and if you don't mix right away you will have pieces of dried egg yolk where all the moisture has been removed by the sugar, so beware.)

Once the milk and cream mixture comes to a boil, pour half into the yolk mixture and whisk together. Pour this back into the remaining milk and cream in the saucepan and heat gently until thickened. In the kitchen we use a thermometer to check when it's ready—183° F is the temperature we take it to (any higher and the egg will scramble, leaving your ice cream lumpy)—but if you don't have one, cook until the mixture coats the back of a wooden spoon and stays there without running right off. Strain the mixture, transfer to another bowl to stop it from cooking, then add the remaining scant 1 cup of milk. It's done this way to maintain a fresh milk flavor. Allow to cool, then churn.

If you don't have an ice-cream machine, freeze the mixture in four batches and, once frozen, blend in a food processor. Return to the freezer after blending.

Next, make the cookies. Preheat your oven to 320° F. Line 2 cookie sheets with nonstick parchment paper.

Cream the butter and sugar together in a bowl, then add the egg, chocolate chips, flour, and baking powder. Stir together until smooth, then roll into golfball-size balls—you should get 16 (2 per person). Arrange them on the prepared cookie sheets leaving room for them to expand, and flatten each one so they are ½ inch thick. Bake for approximately 12 to 15 minutes, then transfer to a rack to cool.

Serve the ice cream in a bowl, with the freshly baked cookies on the side.

Jacek is always making little nibbles to get us through the long days and nights, and this is one of the best yet. It's so easy to make. I would keep this in mind if you find yourself making the peanut brittle or strawberry juice recipes and have a little left over—vanilla ice cream is generally on hand.

# Praline-rolled Ice Cream with Strawberry Juice

**Makes:** 4

**Preparation time:** 10 minutes
(if not using leftovers, 30 minutes
plus freezing)

**Cooking time:** none
(if not using leftovers, 30 minutes)

6 balls of Vanilla Ice Cream
(see page 219)

Peanut Brittle
(see page 168)

2 cups Strawberry Juice
(see page 160)

This will be the shortest method in history. Take a ball of vanilla ice cream, roll it in peanut brittle until completely coated, and place in an espresso cup.

Add 3 tablespoons of strawberry juice, *et voilà*.

Rhubarb and custard hard candies were always a childhood candy-store classic for British children. Here we take the elements and build them up into a knickerbocker-glory style dessert, which looks and tastes amazing. This is one of my mom's favorites, so it had to go into the book. We make the shortbread into perfectly round shapes, so any not used in this recipe will look nice in your cookie jar.

# "Rhubarb and Custard"

**Makes:** 4

**Preparation time:** 1 hour

**Cooking time:** 1 hour 15 minutes

14 ounces Crème Pâtissière (see page 19)

4½ pounds rhubarb, peeled and sliced into ½-inch pieces

¾ cup + 2 tablespoons superfine sugar, divided

1 star anise

3 tablespoons strawberry liqueur

scant 1 cup heavy cream

**For the stock syrup**

2½ cups superfine sugar

2 cups water

juice of ½ a lemon

**For the crème fraîche ice cream**

1¾ cups crème fraîche

2 tablespoons lemon juice

**For the shortbread**

1 stick unsalted butter

heaping ¼ cup superfine sugar, plus extra for sprinkling

1½ cups all-purpose flour

First make the stock syrup. Combine all the ingredients together in a small saucepan and heat until the sugar has dissolved, then let cool.

To make the ice cream, combine the crème fraîche, lemon juice, and 1½ cups stock syrup in a mixing bowl and beat together until well blended. Place in an ice-cream machine and churn until frozen. If you don't have an ice-cream machine, freeze the mixture in a couple of smaller batches, then, when frozen, blend in a food processor and return to the freezer immediately.

If you don't have the crème pâtissière made, now is the time to do it. Follow the steps on page 19.

Next, place the rhubarb in a saucepan with the sugar (reserving 1½ tablespoons for later), the star anise, and liqueur, and enough water to just cover. Bring to a boil, then lower the heat and let simmer for 10 minutes. Strain and let cool. Save the strained syrup and simmer slowly to reduce to a honey-like consistency, then let cool; this will be used to decorate.

To make the shortbread, preheat your oven to 320°F and line a cookie sheet with nonstick parchment paper.

Mix the shortbread ingredients together with your fingers until well combined.

Roll out the mixture to ¼ inch in thickness, then, using a 4-inch cookie cutter, cut out disks and arrange them on the prepared cookie sheet. Keep mixing the trimmings together and rerolling them—there should be zero waste. Place in the fridge to firm up (about 30 minutes), then bake in the oven for approximately 8 minutes, or until golden brown.

Dust with superfine sugar as soon as they come out, and let cool.

Whip the cream and the reserved 1½ tablespoons of sugar to soft peaks, then fold it through the crème pâtissière.

To serve, build up layers of the custard, compote, and slightly crumbled shortbread in a glass, like a sundae, and finish with a good scoop of crème fraîche ice cream and a drizzle of the rhubarb syrup.

SNACKS AND COCKTAILS

Arancini are probably the perfect snack and, with so many variations, I never get bored with them. Originally created as a way to use up leftover risotto in Sicily, the rice is wrapped around a piece of mozzarella, bread-crumbed, and deep-fried. The only challenge I have at home is making sure there is any risotto left! A lot of recipes will call for wine to be added before the stock, and I am one of the few who dislike this. But feel free to add a glass if you like—just make sure you reduce it until almost dry.

# Arancini

**Serves:** 4 as a starter

**Preparation time:** 30 minutes, plus cooling

**Cooking time:** 1 hour

3 tablespoons olive oil

1 onion, minced

1 garlic clove, minced

1 sprig of fresh thyme

1 bay leaf

sea salt and freshly ground black pepper

¾ cup Arborio risotto rice

2 cups hot Chicken Stock (see page 216)

scant 1 cup shelled fresh or frozen peas, defrosted

2 tablespoons unsalted butter

¼ of a bunch of fresh mint, finely chopped

½ cup grated Parmesan cheese

1 ball of mozzarella cheese, cut into ½-inch cubes

heaping ¾ cup all-purpose flour

2 eggs, lightly beaten

1²/₃ cups bread crumbs

vegetable oil, for frying

Heat the olive oil in a skillet, add the onion, garlic, thyme, and bay leaf and cook gently until soft, with no color. Season with salt and pepper. Add the rice and give it a good stir so that it gets slightly sealed by the heat, again with no color.

Slowly start adding the hot stock, just to cover, and cook over medium heat. When it begins to get dry, add more stock and continue in this way until the rice feels cooked. This should take around 20 minutes.

Stir in the peas, then add the butter, mint, and Parmesan and fold in. Remove the thyme and bay leaf and season to taste. Place on a platter to cool, spreading it out as thinly as possible so it cools more quickly.

When the rice has cooled, take a small amount, about half the size of a golfball, wrap it around a cube of mozzarella, and roll it into a tight ball. Repeat with the rest of the rice and mozzarella. Roll the balls in flour, shake off the excess, then dip in the beaten eggs, and finally finish by rolling in the bread crumbs.

At this stage you can refrigerate the arancini for later use—put them into airtight containers, layered on nonstick parchment paper, and they will keep in the fridge for up to 2 days. If you are going to cook them immediately, heat the oil to 350°F in your deep-fat fryer or in a deep heavy saucepan and fry them gently for 3 to 4 minutes. Drain on paper towels, and season lightly with salt to serve.

## VARIATIONS

There are so many possibilities here, the list is endless. Two of my favorites are Pumpkin and Ricotta, and Tomato, Basil, and Mozzarella. Give them a try—they're always a winner.

We spent a good few months working on the recipe for our house bread. A big shout out here to chefs Emilio Solano and Chris Thompson for this development. Emilio took the bread to one level, and then Chris took it to where it is today. When you have perfectionists working with a product day in, day out, they get pretty damn good at it. At the restaurant we have a brick oven. We cook the dough directly on the brick base at a very high temperature, this way the bread cooks super quick. At home, you can either use a ridged grill pan and cook it directly on that, or you can bake the bread in a regular oven. For the plain house bread I'd recommend the grill pan, as essentially it's a variation of a naan dough, and a grill pan really lends itself to this style of bread. For the recipes with toppings, the oven will work best.

# House Breads

**Makes:** 6

**Preparation time:** 20 minutes, plus proving time (approximately 2 hours)

**Cooking time:** 15 minutes

1 cup water, at room temperature

¼ ounce fresh yeast

⅓ cup plain yogurt

3 cups + 2 tablespoons all-purpose flour

1½ teaspoons baking powder

1½ teaspoons sea salt

olive oil, for greasing

Combine the water, yeast, and yogurt in a bowl and let stand at room temperature for 10 minutes. In another bowl, combine the flour, baking powder, and salt.

Add the yeast mixture to the flour mixture and ensure all is incorporated evenly. Continue to knead for 5 minutes in the bowl. Don't be scared if the dough is wet, that's the way it should be. Cover with a wet cloth and let prove for about 2 hours.

When the dough has proved, knock any air out and divide evenly into six balls. You may find that because the dough is quite wet, it's hard to manipulate. Feel free to add a little extra flour to your hands to help. Place the balls of dough on oiled cookie sheets and cover with a dish towel. If not using immediately, place in the fridge at this point.

Preheat your oven to 400°F, or heat a ridged grill pan over medium heat.

When ready to use, take the dough balls out of the fridge and let stand for about 10 to 15 minutes so that they rise again. Pat them down slightly to form a flat surface (about 6 inches in diameter), then either place in the oven for 12 to 15 minutes or, if using a grill pan, oil lightly and grill for 2 to 3 minutes on each side.

**VARIATIONS**

Before baking, after you have flattened the dough balls, add whichever combination of topping ingredients you choose. Here are some of my favorites:

**goat cheese and wild mushrooms (opposite, above)**

**confit garlic and rosemary (opposite, below)**

**caramelized onions, brown anchovy fillets, and capers**

**n'duja and Gruyère**

Having the luxury of a brick oven at the restaurant meant the chefs would inevitably start making themselves pizzas as a snack. Below is our pizza dough recipe, which was created by our Italians. (At one point, around January 2013, we had nine Italians in the kitchen, so you can only imagine.) The different flavor variations below are a reflection of how chefs eat at various times of the day.

# Pizzette

**Makes:** 6
**Preparation time:** 1½ hours
**Cooking time:** 10 to 12 minutes

**For the dough**

3 cups + 2 tablespoons strong white flour, plus extra for dusting

¾ cup semolina flour

2 teaspoons sea salt

½ ounce fresh yeast / 1 sachet of fast-acting instant dry yeast

1¼ cups lukewarm water

3 tablespoons olive oil

**For the topping**

3 tablespoons olive oil, plus extra for greasing

2 onions, minced

4 garlic cloves, minced

2 small dried chiles (optional)

sea salt and freshly ground black pepper

2 x 14-ounce cans of plum tomatoes

1 bunch of fresh basil, roughly chopped

3 balls of mozzarella cheese, the best you can get your hands on

To make the dough, sift the flours together and add the salt. Mix the yeast, water, and oil together in a bowl. Make a well in the flour, and add the yeast liquid. Gradually work the flour and liquid together to form a dough. Continue to knead for 10 minutes, or until the dough is smooth and elastic. Set it aside to rest for 1 hour, or until doubled in size.

On a floured surface, give the dough a small knead to knock the air out of it. If you are planning to use the dough later, seal it in plastic wrap and place it in the fridge. Beware: it will slowly continue to rise.

To make the sauce for the topping, heat the olive oil in a medium saucepan and cook the onions, garlic, and chiles (if using) until soft and translucent. Season with salt and pepper, then add the tomatoes and break them down using a wooden spoon. Bring to a boil, then lower the heat and simmer for 5 minutes. Add the basil and simmer for a further 2 minutes.

Strain the sauce through a sieve, making sure you get as much through as possible. Return to the stove and simmer until reduced by one-quarter. Let cool, then refrigerate if not using immediately.

When ready to cook your pizza, preheat your oven as hot as it will go and line a couple of cookie sheets with oiled nonstick parchment paper. Roll the dough out nice and thin, aiming for the thickness of a dime, give or take, and place it on the prepared cookie sheets. Cover with the tomato sauce, then add as much mozzarella as takes your fancy. Bake for approximately 10 to 12 minutes, or until the dough is cooked and crisp. Note that this varies from oven to oven, so keep a close eye on it.

Finish with torn basil leaves and freshly ground black pepper.

**HERE ARE SOME OF THE VARIATIONS OUR CHEFS EAT...**

**Lewis**—n'duja and Gruyère, with caramelized onions and any chile that's lying around

**Me**—sausage, broccoli, and smoked scamorza

**Francesco**—prosciutto with arugula

**Daniel B**—smoked salmon, poached egg, truffle, and hollandaise (trying to bankrupt us)

This is another great dish for snacking at any time—in the afternoon, predinner, or when you get home late at night—and they also go really well with grilled meats, especially in barbecue season. Once cooked, they keep for a few days, so you can just take them out of the fridge and crisp them in the oven, or in a deep-fat fryer if you have one.

# Polenta Chips with Truffled Pecorino Dip

**Makes:** 18

**Preparation time:** 10 minutes, plus chilling

**Cooking time:** 1½ hours

1 cup milk

1 cup Chicken Stock
(see page 216)

½ cup minced onion

1 bay leaf

2 cloves

⅓ nutmeg, grated

1 cup instant polenta

1 cup grated Parmesan cheese

olive oil or vegetable oil,
for cooking (see method)

1 sprig of fresh rosemary
(optional)

sea salt and freshly ground
black pepper

### For the truffled pecorino dip

⅓ cup Mayonnaise
(see page 217)

3½ ounces aged pecorino cheese,
finely grated

¾ ounce truffle peelings,
finely chopped

2 leaves of fresh chives,
finely chopped

Put the milk, chicken stock, onions, bay leaf, cloves, and nutmeg into a medium saucepan. Bring to just below boiling point, then lower the heat and cook for 30 minutes. Remove the bay leaf and cloves, and add the polenta. Stir well and often, keeping the temperature low enough to stop it from spluttering too much. Within 8 to 10 minutes it should be cooked and smooth. Add the Parmesan and mix well.

Turn out onto a baking pan lined with nonstick parchment paper. The pan should be large enough to allow the polenta to set ¾ inch high. Cover the top directly with plastic wrap, so it's touching, to prevent a skin from forming, and place in the fridge to set.

When chilled and firm, take the polenta out of the fridge and cut it into chips ¾ inch wide and approximately 3¼ inches long (or however long you like).

At this stage you can either lightly coat the chips with olive oil, add some rosemary, and roast in the oven at 350°F for 12 minutes, or until golden. Alternatively, you can deep-fry them for 3 minutes at 340°F until crisp, dropping a sprig of rosemary in there, to serve alongside the chips and dip.

For the dip, mix all the ingredients together. When the chips are cooked, season with salt and pepper, and serve immediately.

These are one of our most successful snacks, in fact, one of the most successful dishes we serve. They are great with a cocktail, a beer, as a snack before dinner, or at 2 A.M., on the way home, or even instead of dessert.

# Barbecue Spiced Pig's Ears

**Serves:** 6 as a snack

**Day 1**
**Preparation time:** 20 minutes
**Cooking time:** 3 hours

**Day 2**
**Preparation time:** 5 minutes
**Cooking time:** 5 minutes

**For the pig's ears**
6 pig's ears, washed
1 onion, peeled
2 stalks of celery
2 carrots, peeled
2 bay leaves
1 sprig of fresh thyme
10 peppercorns
vegetable oil, for deep-frying
all-purpose flour, for dusting
sea salt

**For the spice mix**
½ cup smoked paprika
3 tablespoons onion powder
2 tablespoons garlic powder
2 tablespoons table salt
⅓ cup + 1 tablespoon light brown sugar

## DAY 1

Give the ears a good scrub in cold water. Place them in a saucepan and cover them with cold water. Bring to a boil, then pour off the water and transfer the ears to a clean saucepan. Fill with fresh, clean, cold water and add the whole vegetables, herbs, and peppercorns. Slowly bring to a boil, skimming constantly. Once it is boiling, reduce the heat and let simmer for 3 hours.

Let cool in the cooking liquid, then lift out and place on a baking pan lined with waxed paper. Place another sheet of paper on top, and set another pan on top of that. Place in the fridge, and put anything heavy you may have on top—this could be a few cans or a couple of plates. Let stand in the fridge overnight.

## DAY 2

Heat the oil to 350°F in your deep-fat fryer or in a deep heavy saucepan.

When the ears are cold they will be nice and firm; this makes them much easier to cut. Slice them as thinly as you can, aiming for the thickness of a sheet of paper, and dust with flour. Shake off the excess and place in the fryer for 3 to 4 minutes, or until crisp. Be careful of any spitting fat here, and have a lid or splatter screen ready to set on top of the fryer once the ears go in.

Keep an eye on the temperature of the oil, as it can sometimes drop when you add the ears. If it does, just adjust it up to 375°F so it regulates itself.

Remove from the fryer, place on a plate lined with paper towels to drain any excess oil, then transfer to a mixing bowl. Combine all the spice mix ingredients together. Add 2 teaspoons of the spice mix to the ears and shake them around until all of them are coated, then sprinkle with a little sea salt as well.

Inspired by the snack food, these pork skin "quavers" require a long process of dehydration, but once dry they keep for weeks. As well as a snack, they also work really well as a garnish for any pork dish. Instead of buying a sheet of pork skin, you can just trim the skin off any pork you use and freeze it until you have enough to make a batch. You can also use traditional crackling instead, but this will be much richer.

# Pork Skin "Quavers" with Chile Cream Cheese

**Makes:** 40

**Preparation time:** 12 hours, plus cooling

**Cooking time:** 5 minutes

1 sheet of uncooked pork skin, approximately 18 x 10 inches

vegetable oil, for deep-frying

sea salt

**For the chile cream cheese**

⅓ cup cream cheese

1 chipotle en adobo from a jar, ground to a coarse paste

2 sprigs of fresh cilantro, chopped

2 sprigs of fresh mint, chopped

Wash the pork skin in cold water, then place in a large saucepan and cover with cold water. Bring to a boil, skimming frequently. Once boiling, pour off the water and cover the skin with fresh cold water. Bring to a boil again, then lower the heat and simmer gently for approximately 1 hour. Then, remove from the pan and transfer to a rack to cool.

When cool enough to handle, slice off the layer of fat and any meat still remaining, and then, with a knife blade, continue to scrape as much fat as possible from the skin. Leaving even a little bit behind will stop the skin becoming quaverlike—you need to be left with a sheet of pure skin. Cut into 1-inch squares, and put on a cookie sheet lined with nonstick parchment paper.

Put the squares in the oven at 160°F, or as low as it will go (try to leave the door open a little) and in 12 hours they should become completely hard and dry like little pieces of brown plastic. It helps to press a piece of paper towel on them every couple of hours, to absorb any fat.

When ready to cook, heat the oil to 350°F in a deep-fat fryer or in a deep heavy saucepan. Drop in the little pieces of skin, a few at a time, and watch them puff up within a few minutes to five times their size. You may need to flip them over after 2 minutes so they puff up evenly. Don't be worried if nothing happens for the first 20 to 30 seconds. This is completely normal.

Remove from the fryer or saucepan and place on a plate lined with paper towels. Season with salt. Try playing with different flavored salts, such as chile or lime.

To make the chile cream cheese, put the cream cheese in a bowl and beat in the chipotle chile and chopped herbs. Serve alongside the quavers.

I've always been fascinated with baozi (steamed buns). They are the perfect vehicle for pretty much any slow-cooked meat, or even for fish, such as Singapore chile crab. One day at the restaurant we were playing around with different fillings, and were most satisfied when we tried stuffing them with one of our breakfast components, bacon jam. This was also what made us start playing around with savory doughnuts.

# Bacon Jam Steamed Buns

**Makes:** 24

**Preparation time:** 20 minutes, plus proving

**Cooking time:** 3 hours

### For the steamed buns

3 cups + 2 tablespoons all-purpose flour

heaping ¼ cup superfine sugar

2 teaspoons / 1 x .25-ounce sachet instant active dry yeast

1½ teaspoons baking powder

1 teaspoon salt

scant 1 cup water

3 tablespoons lard, melted

oil, for greasing

### For the bacon jam

1 pound 2 ounces smoked bacon, cut into small lardons

2 onions, minced

2 garlic cloves, minced

2 tablespoons aji panca, or chipotle en adobo from a jar

½ teaspoon smoked paprika

3 tablespoons brown sugar

3 tablespoons dark molasses

⅓ cup cider vinegar

2 shots espresso

You will also need a steamer

To make the bacon jam, put the bacon into a skillet over low heat and cook slowly to render the fat. As the fat melts, pour it away so you have just the meat left. Keep cooking until the bacon starts to caramelize. The brown bits that stick to the bottom are all good, so scrape them off and leave them in the skillet.

Add the onions and garlic, and continue to cook, with no color, until soft. Add the aji panca, smoked paprika, and brown sugar and cook for a further 5 minutes. Add the molasses, vinegar, and espresso and simmer gently until the mixture has a jamlike consistency. This should take an hour or so. Place in a sterilized container, let cool, then cover and refrigerate.

To make the buns, sift the flour into a bowl and mix in the sugar, yeast, baking powder, and salt. Mix the water and lard together, then add to the flour and blend together. Knead for 10 minutes by hand. Place in a clean bowl, cover with a dish towel, and set aside to prove until doubled in size—40 minutes should do.

Knock the air out of the dough and divide it into 24 golfball-size pieces. Let them rest for 5 minutes. Flatten each one into a disk and place a teaspoon of bacon jam inside, then bring up the sides of the dough and seal into a ball. Place each ball on an individual piece of well-oiled nonstick parchment paper, then set aside to prove for 20 minutes.

Place each ball on its paper inside a steamer, 4 at a time. Steam for approximately 12 to 15 minutes and serve immediately.

By **Richard Woods**,
Head of Spirit and Cocktail Development
at Samba Brands Management

# COCKTAILS

I was first introduced to the hospitality industry in 1999, when a new "gastro" bar near my home was looking for bartenders and servers—I still have the recipe cards for the small cocktail list that we were told to learn before we opened. Looking back now, I would say that this point marked the beginning of my hospitality career. A few years later in 2007, and after a move to London, I was heading up the bar at Floridita in London, taking over from legendary bartender Nick Strangeway. This became my introduction to the London bar scene and also to cocktails, and during my time there I continued to learn about spirits, drinks, history, and trends. I visited different cities, both in the UK and abroad, taking notes on my findings for a serve or ideas for flavor pairings.

Since joining Samba Brands Management in 2012, I have worked to create what I refer to as an iconoclastic bar and menu, to illustrate my desire to show how drinking is an experience. I play with flavor pairings and savory elements to show how flavor is as much about aroma as taste—actually, it's more about aroma than about taste. It's also about bridging the gap between food and drink to encapsulate a complete dining experience. You may describe my drinks as weird and quirky, but thought goes into every serve. I take inspiration from all manner of resources: a dinner out, a memorable day, a time of the year, or a personal feeling. I often ask, how can I make a drink better, lighter, fresher, or more flavorful? The following recipes are some that I created prior to Duck & Waffle, some that we have served since opening, and others that are entirely new.

Like many of the drinks in this chapter, the JD & C requires some preparation, in this instance making the cola reduction. The recipe below is for making the cocktail at home and differs slightly from the one we follow in the bar. Among other things, we have chosen here to substitute a more readily available vanilla bean for the very aromatic tonka bean that we usually use. (For a simpler version, you can use cola syrup for a SodaStream and add it directly to the drink.)

# JD & C

**Serves:** 1

**Preparation time:** 45 minutes

**Glass:** stemless wine glass/ old-fashioned glass

1 ¾ ounces Jack Daniels

4 teaspoons salted cola reduction (see below)

1 teaspoon Aperol

1 teaspoon white cacao liqueur

a dash of Angostura bitters

a dash of cider vinegar

ice cubes, to stir and serve

**For the salted cola reduction**
(makes enough for 5 cocktails)

1 ⅓ cups flat cola

1 tablespoon superfine sugar

¼ teaspoon sea salt

½ a vanilla bean

To make the salted cola reduction, put the cola into a saucepan over high heat and let it bubble away until it has reduced to one-third of its original volume. Add the sugar, salt, and half vanilla bean, and cook for a further 20 minutes, stirring. Let cool, then strain into a glass jar or nonreactive container and reserve.

To make your JD&C, stir all the ingredients together with ice cubes and strain into a glass over fresh ice.

This take on a Bellini started life as a completely different cocktail. I first began experimenting with celery in a drink called Astoria, named after the Waldorf Astoria's signature salad—celery, walnuts, and blue cheese (yep)! Looking for something to lift the lighter notes of the celery, I played around with more robust, earthy tastes and found that wasabi worked really well. The blue cheese was dropped, and I ended up with a celery and wasabi Bellini—earthy, fresh, and slightly floral.

# Celery and Wasabi Bellini

To make the celery mix, combine the celery, cucumber, and apple juices in a pitcher or bowl and stir in the sugar syrup and wasabi. Pass through a sieve to get rid of any unwanted fibers, then pour into a glass jar or nonreactive container, put the lid on, and reserve. The mix will keep in the fridge for up to 2 days and will retain its bright color. As soon as it starts to look dull, discard it.

Put the celery mix into a chilled champagne flute, top off with Prosecco, and stir gently.

I love egg white in cocktails. It's a great binder, allowing you to mix and hold all the flavors and add texture. With this sour, I wanted a rich earthiness that would marry well with whiskey. I played around with the flavor of truffle, but it was too overpowering, so I found a way to deliver the aroma of truffle without too much of the flavor—a truffle foam. It was one of the first drinks on Duck & Waffle's cocktail menu and we still make it today.

# Truffle Sour

To make the rosemary-infused whiskey, put the whiskey into a glass jar or nonreactive container with the rosemary sprigs and let infuse for 48 hours.

In the bar we use a whipping canister to make truffle foam, but this simpler all-in-one version also works well. Place the egg white in a shaker and add the truffle oil, lemon juice, and sugar syrup. Shake vigorously for approximately 1 minute. Don't add any ice at this stage. You are looking for a creamy, fluffy texture.

Add the rosemary-infused whiskey to the shaker. Fill with ice and shake again, then strain into a glass over fresh ice.

I first visited New York in 2004, and I found the common pairing of bacon and maple syrup there both weird and totally moreish. A few years later, when I was developing my bartending skills and palate, I remembered this combination of savory and sweet, and the first drink I adapted using this pairing was an Old Fashioned. This has since developed further into the Bacon and Salted Caramel Manhattan.

# Bacon and Salted Caramel Manhattan

**Serves:** 1

**Preparation time:** 3½ hours

**Glass:** chilled Martini/ coupette glass

¼ cup bacon-infused Bourbon (see below)

1 ounce Martini Rosso (sweet vermouth)

½ ounce salted caramel liqueur (see below)

1 teaspoon sugar syrup

2 dashes of Angostura bitters

ice cubes, to stir

**For the bacon infused Bourbon**
(makes enough for 5 cocktails)

8 strips of smoky bacon

12 ounces Bourbon (Woodford Reserve works best)

**For the salted caramel liqueur**
(makes enough for 5 cocktails)

2½ tablespoons superfine sugar

2 teaspoons water

1 teaspoon salt

3½ ounces neutral grain spirit (a vodka at 40% abv works well)

You will also need a sturdy ziplock freezer bag and a sugar thermometer

To make the bacon-infused Bourbon, cook the bacon in a skillet until crisp. Once cooked, turn off the heat and let the bacon rest for a few minutes.

Meanwhile, prepare your homemade water bath. Pour water two-thirds of the way up the sides of a deep saucepan or wok (this is better) and place over medium heat. Do not let the water boil, as this will damage the quality of the alcohol (you want it at a constant 140°F).

Pour the Bourbon into a large, sturdy ziplock freezer bag and add the bacon (complete with any fat and juices). Seal the bag, removing as much air as possible and making sure you don't tear it. Put the bag into your water bath for 55 minutes, then remove and place on a dish towel to dry. Transfer the mixture to a nonreactive container, seal, and place in the freezer for 2 hours.

When you take it out of the freezer you will notice that the freezing process has made the bacon fat separate and solidify, allowing the alcohol to be filtered off cleanly and clearly. Line a funnel or sieve with two-fold muslin (a coffee filter or a dish towel also works well) and put it over an empty glass jar or deep container. Remove the bacon pieces, then strain the liquid through the muslin. This process will take up to 30 minutes. When ready, seal with a lid and reserve.

To make the salted caramel liqueur, put the sugar into a large saucepan over high heat. Allow the sugar to brown and caramelize, then add the water and salt, stirring all the time. Once the sugar has burned and turned to a molasses-like liquid, remove the pan from the heat and add the grain spirit, stirring constantly to prevent the caramel from solidifying. Let cool.

Line a funnel or sieve with two-fold muslin (or a coffee filter or dish towel) and put it over an empty glass jar or deep container. Strain the caramel liquid through the muslin to catch any bits of solidified caramel. This will only take a few minutes. When ready, seal with a lid and reserve.

To make your Manhattan, combine all the ingredients in a mixing glass with ice cubes and stir until icy cold, then strain into a chilled glass.

**Serves:** 1

**Preparation time:** 5 minutes

**Glass:** chilled Martini/ coupette glass

1 lemon wedge

1 ounce gin (45% abv or higher— Plymouth Navy strength works well)

1¾ ounces Martini Rosso (sweet vermouth)

2 bar spoons maraschino liqueur

3 drops of orange bitters (Fee Brothers or Regan's)

1 bar spoon sugar syrup

ice cubes, to stir

The Martinez is by far the simplest cocktail in this book, and shows that elegant and flavorful cocktails can also be simple. Recently I've played with adding a chocolate flavor, which works really well alongside the orange notes of the bitters. When chilled enough, it tastes a little like a Jaffa cake. But I've also experimented with bitters, essence, and a house-made liqueur. Wow! What a combination. The citrus works so well with gin and adds to the vermouth's lift.

# Martinez

Squeeze the juice from the lemon wedge directly into a mixing glass or cocktail shaker. Add the remaining ingredients and ice cubes and stir until icy cold, then strain into a chilled glass.

**Serves:** 1

**Preparation time:** 1 day

**Glass:** chilled Martini/ coupette glass

2¼ ounces vodka (Grey Goose works best)

½ ounce dry vermouth

¼ cup Bloody Mary consommé (see below)

ice cubes, to stir

**For the Bloody Mary consommé** (makes enough for 5 cocktails)

1¾ cups good-quality tomato juice

heaping 1 teaspoon ground black pepper

2 teaspoons crushed pink peppercorns

½ teaspoon sea salt

½ teaspoon celery salt

1 teaspoon Tabasco

1¼ teaspoons Green Tabasco

juice of 1 lemon

3 teaspoons Worcestershire sauce

A Bloody Mary makes a great cocktail. It can be quite filling, though, so I decided to play with its texture, thinning the juice while retaining the flavor. Eventually I achieved a kind of Bloody Mary consommé which, instead of being served long, was strong enough in flavor to be used in small amounts with vodka, gin, or vermouth to make a Martini. Essentially this drink is all in the preparation. Freeze a batch of the Bloody Mary consommé and simply allow it to defrost through muslin or a clean dish towel. The end result is amazingly rich yet lightly textured.

# Essence of Mary

To make the Bloody Mary consommé, pour the tomato juice into a nonreactive container. Add the other ingredients and stir, then let rest for 30 minutes. Seal the container with a lid and place in the freezer overnight.

The next morning, line a funnel or sieve with two-fold muslin (a coffee filter or a dish towel also works well) and put it on top of an empty glass jar or deep container. Strain the frozen tomato mixture through the muslin, allowing it to drip and thaw naturally (this takes several hours). When ready, seal with a lid and reserve.

To make your Essence of Mary, combine all the ingredients in a mixing glass or cocktail shaker with ice cubes and stir, then strain into a chilled glass. Garnish as you wish—try a small dehydrated tomato slice.

I started giving my cocktail menus a savory slant back in 2007, and among the results was a roasted sour: seasoned bone marrow cooked with whiskey, then drip-thawed to separate liquid and fat, producing a flavorful spirit without any oiliness. Fast-forward four years, and on the very first Duck & Waffle menu the bone marrow seasoning was used in a Cosmopolitan. The combination came about through the idea of a Sunday roast, pairing its savoriness and meatiness with the sweetness of an accompanying preserve such as cranberry. It really works.

# Roast Cosmo

**Serves:** 1

**Preparation time:** 3 hours

**Glass:** chilled Martini/coupette glass

3 tablespoons roast cosmo mix (see below)

2½ tablespoons cranberry juice

1 teaspoon lime juice

1 teaspoon lime cordial

1 teaspoon white cacao liqueur

lime wedge or zest, to garnish

ice cubes, to stir

**For the roast cosmo mix**
(makes enough for 5 cocktails)

2 pieces of bone marrow

sea salt and freshly ground black pepper

2 sprigs of fresh rosemary

6 ounces Grey Goose Le Citron vodka

2½ ounces Triple Sec, or other good-quality orange liqueur

You will also need a sturdy ziplock freezer bag and a sugar thermometer

To make the roast cosmo mix, preheat your oven to 400°F. Put the bone marrow in a roasting pan, season with salt and pepper, and add a couple of rosemary sprigs. Place in the oven for 20 to 25 minutes, or until the marrow is cooked through. Remove from the oven and let it rest for a few minutes.

Meanwhile, prepare your homemade water bath. Pour water two-thirds of the way up the sides of a deep saucepan or wok (this is better) and place over medium heat. Do not let the water boil, as this will damage the quality of the alcohol (you want it at a constant 140°F).

Put the vodka and Triple Sec into a large sturdy ziplock freezer bag and add the roasted bone marrow complete with the herbs and any juices. Seal the bag, removing as much air as possible and making sure no sharp pieces of bone can tear it. Put the bag into your water bath and leave for 45 minutes, then remove and place on a dish towel to dry. Transfer the mixture to a nonreactive container, seal with a lid, and place in the freezer for 2 hours.

When you take it out of the freezer you will notice that the freezing process has made the bone marrow fat separate and solidify, allowing the alcohol to be filtered off cleanly and clearly. Line a funnel or sieve with two-fold muslin (a coffee filter or a dish towel also works well) and put it on top of an empty glass jar or deep container. Remove the marrow pieces first, then strain the liquid through the muslin. This process will take up to 30 minutes. When ready, seal the container with a lid and reserve.

To make your Roast Cosmo, shake all the ingredients except the garnish with ice cubes and double strain into a chilled glass. Garnish with a lime wedge or zest.

**Left to right:** Cereal Killer Old-Fashioned, Prairie Provençal, Roast Cosmo

This one is for the kids among us. Chocolate rice pops is such a great cereal—malty, chocolatey—and for me, a bowlful with some ice-cold milk still brings back happy childhood memories. You can capture this nostalgic flavor by adding the cereal to a glass of Bourbon. I investigated various cereals but found that my favorite worked best. The only problem I've encountered is that I find my days are a lot slower if I start the morning with more than one of these!

# Cereal Killer Old-Fashioned

**Serves:** 1

**Preparation time:** 3½ hours to 3 days

**Glass:** large old-fashioned glass

¼ cup chocolate rice pop-infused Bourbon (see below)

2 teaspoons sugar syrup

2 dashes of Angostura bitters

ice cubes, to stir and serve

**For the chocolate rice pop-infused Bourbon**
(makes enough for 5 cocktails)

14 ounces chocolate-flavored rice pop cereal

14 ounces Bourbon (Woodford Reserve works best)

You will also need a sturdy ziplock freezer bag and a sugar thermometer

In the bar we use the sous-vide method to make the infused Bourbon, but there are two alternative methods that I have found work well at home. The first is the lazy approach and requires more infusing time. The second is quicker but requires more attention. Note: The reason for the higher volume of alcohol used in this recipe is due to the absorption of the chocolate-flavored rice cereal. Once you strain off the liquid, you will find that you lose up to 15 percent.

**METHOD 1**
Put the cereal into a glass jar or nonreactive container and cover with the Bourbon. Seal with a lid and let stand for a minimum of 72 hours, or until you are happy with the results, periodically tasting (remember to gently shake the jar or container every now and again, to release more flavor). Once you are happy with your infusion, line a funnel or sieve with two-fold muslin (a coffee filter or a dish towel also works well) and put it on top of an empty glass jar or deep container. Strain the mixture through the muslin. When ready, seal with a lid and reserve.

**METHOD 2**
Meanwhile, prepare your homemade water bath. Pour water two-thirds of the way up the sides of a deep saucepan or wok (this is better) and place over medium heat. Do not let the water boil, as this will damage the quality of the alcohol (you want it at a constant 140°F).

Put the bourbon and cereal into a large ziplock freezer bag and seal, removing as much air as possible and being careful not to tear the bag. Put the bag into your water bath and leave for 1 hour, then remove and place on a dish towel to cool. Transfer the mixture to a nonreactive container, seal with a lid, and place in the freezer for 2 hours.

When you take it out, you will notice that the freezing process has made the cereal solidify, allowing the alcohol to be filtered off cleanly and clearly. Line a funnel or sieve with two-fold muslin (a coffee filter or a dish towel also works well) and put it on top of an empty glass jar or deep container. Strain the liquid through the muslin. This process will take up to 30 minutes. When ready, seal with a lid and reserve.

To make your Cereal Killer Old-Fashioned, combine all the ingredients in a mixing glass with ice cubes and stir until icy cold, then strain into an iced-filled glass.

**Serves**: 1

**Preparation time:** 5 minutes

**Glass:** chilled small tasting glass or liqueur glass

1 duck egg yolk

1¾ ounces Bombay Sapphire gin

2 teaspoons tomato ketchup

2 tablespoons tomato juice

a pinch of salt

a pinch of black pepper

a dash of balsamic vinegar

micro cilantro leaves, to garnish (optional)

ice cubes, to stir

When creating a drink, it's important to think about why you are doing it—it might be meant as a drink to have on its own, or it might be intended to accompany food, without taking away from the food itself. This little cocktail was created for sipping with oysters. It's powerful and strong, so you only need to serve it in small tasting measures. The sharpness of the ketchup and the calmness of the cilantro work well with the gin.

# Prairie Provençal

Place the yolk in the bottom of your glass.

Shake the remaining ingredients, apart from the micro cilantro, with ice cubes and double strain into your glass, on top of the yolk. Garnish with micro cilantro leaves, if you like.

This cocktail is inspired by the most quintessential flavors of the sea and is one of the best pairings.

# Perle de Mer

**Serves:** 1

**Preparation time:** 1 day

**Glass:** chilled Martini glass

1¾ ounces Grey Goose vodka

2 tablespoons "sea spray" vermouth (see below)

1 teaspoon olive jus

ice cubes, to stir and serve

1 caper berry, to garnish

**For the "sea spray" vermouth** (makes enough for 5 cocktails)

4¼ ounces Noilly Prat vermouth

1 freshly shucked oyster shell

To make the "sea spray" vermouth, put the Noilly Prat into a nonreactive container and add the oyster shell. Let stand overnight to infuse.

The following morning, line a funnel or sieve with two-fold muslin (a coffee filter or a dish towel also works well) and set it on top of an empty jar or nonreactive container. Discard the oyster shell and strain the vermouth through the muslin.

To make your Perle de Mer, combine all the ingredients in a mixing glass with ice cubes and stir until icy cold, then strain into a chilled glass and garnish with a caper berry.

# RECIPE BASICS

## CHICKEN STOCK

**Makes:** 2 pints

3 chicken carcasses
1 onion, peeled and halved
1 stalk of celery
1 leek, halved
1 bay leaf
10 black peppercorns
1 sprig of fresh thyme

Place all the ingredients in a large saucepan, leaving the vegetables in whole pieces (halves where stated) so that they don't break down as the stock cooks. Cover with cold water, then slowly bring to a boil, skimming off any fat or foam as they arise. Lower the heat and let simmer for 3 hours. The more fat and impurities you manage to remove, the clearer, and therefore purer, your stock will be.

At the end of the 3 hours, strain the stock through a sieve lined with a fine cloth, by slowly pouring it through—don't press anything or it will become cloudy. Pour into a clean saucepan and simmer until reduced by half. Strain again and chill.

## BRINE

**Makes:** 2 pints

2 pints water
¼ cup sea salt
20 peppercorns
2 bay leaves
5 juniper berries
20 coriander seeds

Bring the water to a boil in a large saucepan, then turn the heat off. Add the salt, let it dissolve, then add the rest of the ingredients and let cool.

When cold, the brine is ready to use.

## PICKLING LIQUID

**Makes:** 1¼ cups

scant 1 cup white wine vinegar
scant ½ cup water
½ cup less 2 tablespoons superfine sugar
½ tablespoon salt
a pinch of coriander seeds
a pinch of black peppercorns
1 bay leaf

Put all the ingredients into a large saucepan and bring to a boil, then strain and let cool.

To use, put whatever ingredients you want to pickle into sterilized jars, pour in the pickling liquid, and seal the jars tightly.

## SHERRY DRESSING

**Serves:** 2 to 3

3 tablespoons olive oil
3 tablespoons sherry vinegar

Put the olive oil and sherry vinegar into a bowl and whisk together. Don't worry if it separates when you set it aside—just give it a whisk again before you need to use it.

## BALSAMIC GLAZE

**Makes:** scant 1 cup

2 cups good-quality
balsamic vinegar

Put the vinegar into a saucepan over medium heat and let simmer until it has reduced by half and has a consistency like liquid honey. This should take around 20 minutes but be careful, as it goes from honey to burned in seconds.

Toward the end, give the vinegar a swirl or a stir every couple of minutes, as this is when the sugars begin to thicken and it may start to stick to the bottom of the pan.

## CONFIT SHALLOTS

**Makes:** approximately 3½ ounces

1¼ cups olive oil
pinch of salt
5 banana shallots, finely diced

Put the oil, salt, and shallots into a saucepan and heat gently for 30 minutes, or until the shallots are soft with no color.
This will keep, covered with the oil, for up to a week.

## CONFIT GARLIC

**Makes:** approximately 18 cloves

3 heads of garlic, broken into
cloves (not peeled)
1¼ cups olive oil

Put the garlic cloves into a saucepan, cover with the olive oil, and heat gently for 30 minutes, or until the garlic is soft. Be careful not to let it color.

Store the cloves in the oil, which is great to use on its own, on pizza, or on salads.

## MAYONNAISE

**Makes:** 1¾ cups

2 egg yolks
1 tablespoon Dijon mustard
3 tablespoons white wine vinegar
1¾ cups peanut oil
sea salt and freshly ground
white pepper

In a food processor, blend the egg yolks, mustard, and vinegar together. Slowly start adding the oil, and if the mixture doesn't continue to blend together, slow the machine down a little.
If the mixture becomes too thick and excessively greasy, add warm water, a teaspoonful at a time, until it loosens up a bit. Season with salt and pepper.

## DUCK CURE

**Makes:** 12 ounces

²/₃ cup salt
¾ cup + 2 tablespoons superfine sugar
½ tablespoon orange zest
a pinch of ground cinnamon
1 clove
1 star anise
5 pink peppercorns
1 tablespoon brandy

Mix all the ingredients together and store sealed in an airtight container.

## STANDARD CURE

**Makes:** 2¾ ounces (scant ½ cup)

¼ cup sea salt
2 tablespoons sugar
2 sprigs of fresh thyme, leaves picked
10 black peppercorns
1 star anise

Mix all the ingredients together and store sealed in an airtight container.

## GRANOLA

This makes quite a lot, and it's a great ingredient to have in your cupboard. You can easily halve the quantities if you want to make a smaller amount.

**Makes:** 2¼ pounds

1 pound 2 ounces oats
¾ cup hazelnuts
¾ cup almonds
¾ cup pistachios
1 cup pecan halves
3 tablespoons sesame seeds
3 tablespoons sunflower seeds
3 tablespoons pumpkin seeds
½ cup less 2 tablespoons light corn syrup
⅓ cup honey
1 cup less 2 tablespoons raisins
1 scant cup dried apricots

Preheat your oven to 320°F.

Put all the ingredients except the dried fruit into a bowl and stir to combine. Divide the mixture between 2 large lipped baking pans lined with nonstick parchment paper. Bake in the oven for 40 minutes, giving the mixture a stir every 10 minutes, so it all becomes evenly colored.

Remove from the oven, stir in the dried fruit, and let cool.

## HONEYCOMB

When adding the baking soda, do be aware that it rises and expands very quickly—be ready!

**Makes:** 1 medium baking pan

2½ tablespoons honey
¼ cup water
⅓ cup glucose
1½ cups + 2 tablespoons superfine sugar
2 tablespoons baking soda

You will also need a candy thermometer

Line a deep roasting pan with nonstick parchment paper.

Put all the ingredients except for the baking soda into a large saucepan over medium heat. Let the sugar dissolve, then continue to cook until a temperature of 311 °F is reached on a candy thermometer.

Remove from the heat and add the baking soda. Whisk well, then pour into the prepared pan. Let cool and set.

When cool and firm, smash the honeycomb into smaller pieces. Store sealed in an airtight container for up to 2 to 3 weeks.

## VANILLA ICE CREAM

**Makes:** 2 pints

2 cups milk
2 cups heavy cream
seeds from 1 vanilla bean
scant 1 cup superfine sugar
10 egg yolks

Bring the milk, cream, and vanilla to a boil in a large saucepan. Meanwhile, put the sugar and egg yolks into a bowl and whisk very well. (Sugar absorbs moisture, and if you don't mix straight away you will have pieces of dried egg yolk where all the moisture has been removed by the sugar, so beware.)

Once the milk and cream mixture comes to a boil, pour half into the yolk mixture and whisk together. Pour this back into the remaining milk and cream in the saucepan and heat gently until thickened. In the kitchen we use a thermometer to check once it is cooked (183 °F is the temperature we take it to—any higher and the egg will scramble, leaving your ice cream lumpy), but if you don't have one, cook until it coats the back of a wooden spoon and stays there without running right off. Strain the mixture, transfer to another bowl to stop it from cooking, then cool and churn.

If you don't have an ice-cream machine, freeze the mixture in four batches and, once frozen, blend in a food processor. Return to the freezer after blending.

# INDEX

**almonds** 19, 166
Ansell, Dominique 19
apricot jam 102
arancini 186–7
artichokes, globe
    with Caerphilly crumble 60–1
    vignole with pork belly 147
artichokes, Jerusalem
    with monkfish & salsify 135
    and truffle ravioli 152–3
asparagus
    with crispy chicken skin & confit egg yolk 62–3
    grilled, with pink grapefruit sauce 64–5
avocado, Colombian eggs 20

**bacon**
    baked cod & clam chowder 132
    butter, with grilled oysters 81
    custard 177
    in hangover pizza 44
    jam, steamed buns 200–1
    with mackerel, split peas & mint 136
    in roasted artichokes 60
    & salted caramel Manhattan 208
bagna cauda, with cauliflower 67
baked Alaska 160–1
Balloo, Timon 8–9, 140
balsamic glaze 53, 70–1, 217
banana 16, 18, 30–1
beans on toast 32–3
beef
    carpaccio with foie gras 100–1
    Leo Sayer burger 43
beets
    & celeriac relish with mutton faggots 148–9
    with goat curd, honeycomb & watercress 54–5
Bellini, celery & wasabi 204–5
Billera, Danielle 6, 9
Bloody Mary consommé 209
blueberry coulis 76
Bokovza, Shimon 6–8, 9
Bourbon 208, 212
brandade, whipped, with charred tomato jam 94–5
bread
    house breads 188–9
    pudding, chocolate 176–7
    *see also* brioche
brine 216
brioche
    with duck eggs 28–9
    Leo Sayer burger 43
    smoky mutton Sloppy Joe 46–7
    toasted PBJ with banana & berries 30–1
broccoli
    with Caesar dressing 56
    pizzette 190

brownies, peanut butter ice cream & marshmallow 156–8
buns
    brioche 43, 46–7
    steamed, with bacon jam 200–1
burgers
    Leo Sayer 42–3
    mutton, harissa-spiced, with lime crème fraîche 104–5

**cake**, pistachio & olive oil with Chantilly cream 174–5
capers 78, 94
carpaccio 100–1, 112–13
carrots
    with honey-glazed ham hock 144
    slow-roasted, with lardo, peas & mint 68–9
cauliflower, roasted, with bagna cauda & pickled walnuts
    66–7
celeriac & beet relish 148
celery & wasabi bellini 204–5
Cereal Killer Old-Fashioned 212
cheese
    Caerphilly 60
    Cheddar 33, 44
    chile cream 199
    Fourme d'Ambert 173
    Gruyère 24, 28, 36, 43, 190
        mozzarella 44, 187, 190
    parmesan 40, 73, 116, 150, 153, 187, 193
    pecorino 100, 150, 153, 193
    ricotta 40
    taleggio 48
cherry cola float 159
chicken
    necks, crispy, with chile & garlic 114–15
    roast Sunday 138–9
    skin
        crispy, with asparagus 63
    gravy 138
    stock 216
chips, polenta 192–3
chocolate
    bread pudding with bacon custard 176–7
    brownies with peanut butter ice cream & marshmallow
      156–8
    chip cookies 178–80
    cocoa almonds 166
    deep-fried, with malt ice cream & oat crunch 170–1
    hazelnut spread 18
    salted caramel truffles 167
chorizo 23, 36, 78–9
chutney, beer 106–7
clams
    with baked scallops 96
    chowder, with baked cod & bacon 132–3
    in dayboat fish stew 128
    & mussels, with n'duja & fennel broth 92–3
    steamed, with guanciale, lardo & parsley crumb 98–9

cocktails 202–15
cod
    with clam chowder & bacon 132–3
    in dayboat fish stew 128
    salt cod in brandade 94–5
cola
    cherry cola float 159
    salted 203
compote, fruit 14
confit
    egg yolk 63
    garlic 217
    shallots 217
cookies & milk ice cream 178–80
corn on the cob, with jerk spices & coconut 57
crab, roasted claws, with garlic butter 82–3
crème pâtissière 19, 168, 183
croissants, dossants 19
crunch 18, 19, 171
cucumber, pickled 90
cures 218
custard
    bacon 177
    Grand Marnier 163
    with rhubarb 183
cuttlefish risotto & fennel 88–9

**Doherty**, Daniel, philosophy 10
dossants, coffee & amaretto 17, 19
doughnut, spicy ox cheek, with apricot jam 102–3
dressings 56, 216
drinks
    cherry cola float 159
    cocktails 202–15
duck
    cure 218
    & waffle, with mustard maple syrup 140–1
Duck & Waffle, background 6–11

**Eccles** cake, Fourme d'Ambert 172–3
eggplant, smoky purée 110
eggs
    Colombian 20–1
    confit yolk 62–3
    duck
        in brioche basket 28–9
        with duck & waffle 140–1
        en cocotte, with mushrooms & Gruyère cheese 24–5
        Prairie Provençal 213
    fried, with pearl barley ragout 22–3
    in hangover hash 36–7
    in hangover pizza 44
    poached
        with London Particular 120–1
        with salt beef hash 34
        with smoked haddock chowder 84, 86

endive marmalade 122–3
Essence of Mary cocktail 209

**faggots**, mutton, with beet & celeriac relish 148–9
fava beans, in vignole 147
fennel
    with cuttlefish risotto 88–9
    with meatballs & ricotta 40
    & n'duja broth with mussels & clams 92–3
    pickled 48
fish stew, seared dayboat, with spring vegetables 128–9
fishballs, with lobster cream 72–3
flatbreads 188
foie gras 100–1, 119
food philosophy 10
fritto misto, piggy 116–17

**garlic**
    butter, with crab claws 82
    confit 217
gin 209, 213
goat curd 23, 54–5
granola 218
    with ricotta & lemon 52–3
    with yogurt & compote 14–15
grapefruit, pink 64
gravy, chicken skin 138
guanciale, with steamed clams 99

**haddock**, smoked
    chowder with poached egg & puffed rice 84, 86
    with duck eggs en cocotte 24
    with hash browns & mustard cream 26–7
    Scotch egg with curried mayonnaise 85, 87
halibut tartare with blueberries & pickled mushrooms 76–7
ham hock
    with beans 33
    with carrots & turnips 142–4
    London Particular 120
    with suckling pig 145
hangover
    hash 36–7
    pizza 44–5
hash browns with haddock 26–7
hazelnut, chocolate spread 18
Henderson, Fergus 10
hollandaise 34
honeycomb 54, 156, 219

**ice** cream
    baked Alaska, with strawberry juice 160–1
    cherry cola float 159
    crème fraîche, with rhubarb 182–3
    malt, with deep-fried chocolate 170–1
    milk, with cookies 178–80
    peanut butter, with brownies 156–8

praline-rolled, with strawberry juice  181
    with roasted peaches  164
    vanilla  219
ingredients  10

**Jack** Daniels, JD & C  203
Johnson, Matthew  6

**lamb**
    crispy, with mutton Sloppy Joe  46–7
    hara bhara, with eggplant & mint yogurt  110–11
lardo
    & parsley crumb with steamed clams  99
    with slow-roasted carrots  68–9
    vignole with pork belly  147
lemon
    candied  53
    marshmallows  166
lentils, with sausage rolls  119
lime, crème fraîche  105
lobster cream sauce, with fishballs  72–3
London Particular  120–1

**macaroons**, PBJ  168
mackerel
    split peas, mint & bacon  136–7
    tartare with smoked vodka & pickled cucumber  90
Manhattan, bacon & caramel  208
maple syrup, mustard  140
marshmallows  156, 166
Martinez cocktail  209
Martini  208, 209
mayonnaise  87, 217
meatballs, with fennel & ricotta  40–1
meringue, Italian  160–1, 168
monkfish, roast, with salsify & Jerusalem artichokes  134–5
mushrooms
    pickled  76
    trompette, with monkfish  135
    wild
        with duck egg en cocotte  24
        with pearl barley ragout  23
        with suckling pig  145
mussels
    with baked scallops  96
    & clams with n'duja & fennel broth  92–3
    in dayboat fish stew  128
mustard  27, 140
mutton
    faggots, with beet & celeriac relish  148–9
    harissa-spiced slider with lime crème fraîche  104–5
    Sloppy Joe with crispy lamb breast  47

**n'duja**  92–3, 190
Newborough, Lord  10
Noble Rot  100

**oatcakes**  170–1
octopus, roasted, with chorizo, potato & caper berries  78–9
Old Brewery, Greenwich  106
onion jam  36
orange, steamed puddings with Grand Marnier custard  162–3
ox cheek
    with cheese sandwich  48–9
    doughnut with apricot jam  102–3
oysters, broiled, with spicy bacon butter  80–1

**paprika**, smoked, sugar  102
pasta
    Jerusalem artichoke and truffle ravioli  152–3
    rabbit agnoli, with sage brown butter  150–1
peach, roasted, with thyme, honey & saffron sponge  164–5
peanut
    brittle  168, 181
    butter
        ice cream with brownies  156–8
        mousse  168
        PBJ macaroons  168–9
        toasted PBJ  30
    crunch  18
pear with venison carpaccio  112
pearl barley ragout, with goat curd & fried egg  22–3
peas
    in arancini  187
    with baked sea bass  126
    with carrots & lardo  68
    in London Particular  120–1
    split, with mackerel, mint & bacon  136–7
peperonata  58–9
    in hangover hash  36
    in hangover pizza  44
    with pearl barley ragout  23
Perle de Mer cocktail  214–15
pickling liquid  216
pig's ears *see* pork
pistachio & olive oil cake with Chantilly cream  174–5
pizza  44–5, 190–1
polenta chips with truffled pecorino dip  192–3
pollock fishballs, with lobster cream & Parmesan  72–3
pork
    belly
        with endive marmalade, orange & walnuts  122–3
        slow-braised, with vignole  146–7
    guanciale  99
    meatballs, with fennel & ricotta  40–1
    piggy frito misto  116–17
    pigs' ears, spiced  194–5
    pork skin "Quavers" with chile cream cheese  198–9
    sausage rolls with prunes & lentils  118–19
    suckling pig, slow-roasted, with mushrooms & barley  145

potatoes
    with baked sea bass  126
    hangover hash  36–7
    hash browns  26–7
    mashed, with scallops  96
    with octopus & chorizo  78–9
    roast  138
    salt beef hash  34–5
    whipped brandade  94–5
Prairie Provençal  213
prunes, with sausage rolls  119

**rabbit**
    agnoli, with sage butter  150–1
    rillettes, with chutney  106–7
ravioli  152–3
rhubarb, and "custard"  182–3
Rhug Estate  10
rice
    arancini  186–7
    pops, in cocktail  212
    puffed, with smoked haddock chowder  84, 86
ricotta
    with granola & lemon  52–3
    with meatballs & fennel  40
rillettes, rabbit, with beer chutney  106–7
risotto, cuttlefish, with charred fennel  88–9
River Café  150
Roast Cosmo cocktail  210–11

**sage** butter  150
salsify, with monkfish & Jerusalem artichokes  135
salt beef hash & poached eggs  34–5
salt cod, in brandade  94–5
salt-baking  130–1, 143, 144
salted caramel  167, 208
Samba Brands Management  6, 8, 202
sandwich, grilled cheese, with oxtail & pickled fennel  48–9
sausage rolls, with prunes & lentils  118–19
Sayer, Leo  43
scallops, baked  96–7
Scotch egg, smoked haddock, with curried mayonnaise  85, 87
sea bass
    baked whole with zucchini, potatoes & peas  126–7
    in dayboat fish stew  128
sea bream, salt-baked  130–1
seaweed butter sauce  131
shallots, confit  217
sherry dressing  216
shortbread  183
sliders, mutton, harissa-spiced, with lime crème fraîche  104–5
Sloppy Joe, smoky mutton  47
soup
    London Particular  120–1
    n'duja & fennel broth  93

sponge  160, 164–5
standard cure  218
steamed buns, bacon jam  200–1
steamed puddings, orange, with Grand Marnier custard  162–3
strawberry juice  160, 181
stuffings  138, 145
suckling pig, slow-roasted, with mushrooms & barley  145
sugar, smoked paprika  102
Sugarcane Raw Bar Grill  6, 8–9, 20
Sushi Samba  6, 9

**tomatoes**
    Bloody Mary consommé  209
    with grilled asparagus  64–5
    jam, with brandade  94–5
    peperonata  58–9
    pizzette  190–1
    Prairie Provençal  213
Triple Sec, Roast Cosmo  210–11
truffle sour cocktail  204
truffles, salted caramel  167
truffles, savory  152–3, 192–3
tuna, with watermelon, balsamic glaze & basil  70–1
turnips, salt-baked  143, 144

**van** Horne, Harriet  10
venison carpaccio, with pear, almonds & pine embers  112–13
vermouth  208, 209, 214
vignole, with pork belly  147
vodka  90, 209, 210–11, 214–15

**waffles**
    & duck, with mustard maple syrup  140–1
    sweet Belgian  16, 18
walnuts  67, 122
watercress  52–3, 54–5
watermelon, with tuna  70
whiskey, truffle sour  204
Wilson, Zeren  43
Woods, Richard  202

**yogurt**
    granola & compote  14–15
    mint  110

**zucchini**, with sea bass  126

## AUTHOR'S ACKNOWLEDGMENTS

This page is often the last piece of text to be written, which seems wrong, but, having seen the sheer amount of work that goes into writing a book, and all the wonderful people involved, I now appreciate how many people I would have missed, and I'm glad that I am able to thank everyone who has made this happen.

I don't have the talents to write a speech, nor enough ways to say, "I'd like to thank…" and, as a life-long list-writer, I'm going to list it out and pray I haven't forgotten anyone.

Maureen Mills, for introducing me to the wonderful Alison Starling, who, between them, made this dream come true and have guided me at every stage.

Samba Brands Management, for giving me this opportunity to fulfill my dream and for letting me do it my way.

Everyone at Octopus Publishing, especially Sybella, Juliette & Katherine for sharing their expertise.

Anders Schønnemann. He's the guy who took the photos that took my breath away, a huge talent, and a great man who we were very lucky to have, and his "always hungry" assistant Louise.

Annie Rigg, for making my recipes look fantastic. I cannot portray how impressed I was with not only her supreme level of cooking, but the eye for food styling. Another level, and I'd give her any job in my kitchen.

Kat Mead, recipe tester extraordinaire. She helped translate chef speak into normal comprehensible English, which is no easy task, let me tell you.

All of our suppliers for helping out, including Simpsons, Rhug Estate, Parsley in Time, Flour Station, and Nisbets.

Billingsgate Market, for allowing us to get messy taking pictures of fish.

The kitchen team at the restaurant, led by Tom Cenci, my best friend and life-saver—nothing would have been possible without his support. I am forever in his debt for how he has helped me at D&W. Jacek, Kamil, Francesco, Janos & Daniel, together with Tomek, Chris, Michael, David W, Manny, Seb, Jon, Billy, Lewis, Ewa, Tammy, Borja, Junior, Luca, Suza, Pedro, Matt, Yamil, Andrea, Jorge, David A, and Rafael, thank you all guys.

Thanks to Chan and Richard for their expertise on the desserts and drinks respectively.

All of our guests and friends on social media for being so supportive, whether telling us what you love, or even what you don't. That's the only way we learn and thank you for being so honest.

And last, but not least, I'd like to thank Marcella, my beautiful wife. Being a chef's wife is a huge sacrifice, one that she never complains about. She has shown nothing but support for my career during the 10 years we have known each other, and I am incredibly lucky to have her in my life. That is something I will never forget. Thank you thank you thank you.